I0069840

The

Book
Book

A Complete Guide
to
Creating a Book
On Your Computer

THIRD EDITION

Revised and Expanded

by

Lily Splane

Anaphase II Publishing
A DIVISION & IMPRINT OF CYBERLEPSY MEDIA
WWW.CYBERLEPSY.COM

The *Book* Book:
A Complete Guide to Creating a Book on Your Computer

THIRD EDITION

Copyright © 1995–2014 Lily Splane

ISBN 13: 978-0-945962-44-1
ISBN 10: 0-945962-44-4

No part of this work may be reproduced in any form—
existing or to be developed in the future—
without the express written permission of the author/publisher.

Published in the United States of America

Colophon: This book was electronically typeset in 11-point Garamond and Helvetica.

Anaphase II Publishing
A DIVISION & IMPRINT OF CYBERLEPSY MEDIA
4669 Cherokee Avenue, Suite E
San Diego, CA 92116-3654
WWW.CYBERLEPSY.COM

Dedication

For Penny Duitsman and Sandy Schiefer

What would I be doing with my life right now,
if it were not for you clowns?

Contents

Preface

Welcome, do-it-yourselfers!

You're probably reading this book because you've come to the profound realization that making money with your book requires that it be *published* and made available to the public. Many frustrating years and a bloated folder of rejection slips are not pathways to publishing bliss.

Take charge and take heart. You *can* do it yourself *and* you can do it *right*—creating books indistinguishable in quality and value from any paperback book released by the Big Guys.

Thirty-plus years as a free-lance writer, editor, and book production specialist for independent publishers have resulted in this manual—a veritable memory dump of everything critical to producing your own book. It is far from everything I know about book production, as much of what I've learned is borderline useless, not only because it isn't critical, but because most of what I know is doomed to become obsolete as the publishing industry evolves.

Given enough time, everything within these pages is destined to become archaic spooge. But, I expect bookmaking will be pretty much the same for at least the next five to eight years. So dive in confidently.

This book is decidedly computer-oriented. Bookmaking on computer is such a pleasure, I can't conceive of having to go back to the bad old days of light tables, Exacto® knives, and mucilage glue, much less to meticulously hand-placing metal type between rows of hot lead in a wooden gutter tray. Though you can make a book with any high-end word processor (with limitations), I have made numerous references to Adobe InDesign®, the current ultimate page-layout and book-production program for Windows and Macintosh. InDesign® is the publishing altar at which I worship daily. I've even been caught chanting kerning tables in my sleep.

I've written this book in the simplest, most descriptive prose of which I am capable. Chances are, if you're not already initiated into the dark underworld of computer graphics, you'll get a brain cramp on such topics as scan resolution and color separations. As it is, I'm just coming out of the mini-stroke I had while writing these sections.

The Book Book was designed to make book planning, typesetting, layout, and prepress production *accessible to* and *easy for* anyone with computer experience. If it turns out that's not the case for you, I'm always available for consultations and contracts. Bring dead presidents.

Lily Splane
September, 2014

Lily Splane

Acknowledgements

I'd like to thank Theresa Freese for her additional editing.
There is nothing quite so valuable to a writer or an editor, as another editor's eyes.

Introduction

The *Book Book* promises to take you from scratching your head to confidently flouncing into bookstores with your books in arm. Pay attention—I've left nothing out, but at the same time have added nothing that will get in the way of your goal: getting your own book to press and into the buyers' hands in just a few months.

Making your book marketable entails complying with some oftentimes rigid industry standards. If you are a writer, at least half of the problem is solved; you know what good writing is. If you've done any free-lance editing, all the better for your own book—your eye will be more discerning.

The book industry demands not only competent writing, but an attractive and durable format for your book. There are *standards* for book size, kind of paper, kind of printing, kind of type, margins, cover design, pricing, and discounts. Very little deviation from industry standards is tolerated. If you don't observe what is expected of you, you won't sell your books.

Of the hundreds of small publishers that start up each year, two-thirds go belly-up within a year—almost always because of poor planning and below-standard products.

I get hundreds of pieces of mail each month from small presses and publishers (though *small press* and *publisher* are often used interchangeably, I will use the word *publisher* to refer to those enterprises that produce books for sale, and *press* to indicate those that print books in volume for publishers). I am always appalled at the quality of brochures, newsletters, and even books released by these businesses. Though printed on nice paper and sometimes in full color, nothing can rescue a piece that is fraught with misspelled words, bad grammar and punctuation, sloppy typesetting, and garnished with a dozen fonts and type sizes. My hair stands on end while wading through foot and inch marks passing for quotes, misplaced apostrophes, a space-hyphen-space in lieu of a proper *em* dash, and hyphens in number ranges instead of *en* dashes. These beautifully printed pieces shout *amateur* and *ignoramus* to those who know better.

Your book doesn't have to be among the volumes of poorly-designed printed matter. Your book can stand out and command respect, even awe.

In *The Book Book* you will learn:

- What kinds and sizes of type are expected in books
- How to use typography and design to enhance the appearance of your book and make it shout *professional* from the very first page
- What the margins should measure
- What binding is ideal for your book
- How to design an irresistible cover that will make people want to open your book
- How to scan art into your book
- How many pages your book should have
- How to set up a book in signatures
- What kind of paper to use for your book
- How to decide on a cover price
- How to register your book into international databases and the Library of Congress
- How to ask for and get exactly what you want from your printing press
- How to approach distributors and bookstores, and what discounts to give them
- What *never* to do in a book that turns booksellers off
- How to ship books
- How to collect payments

In short, unless revealed otherwise, your books and your business practices will appear in all ways like those of a large book publisher, and you will be treated with the respect due you.

Self-publishing encompasses three immutable certainties: It's hard work, it's not cheap, and it's very gratifying. If you do what it takes, a fourth certainty can be yours: *It's profitable!*

Part 1

Planning Stages

The Publishing Game

According to the North American Bookdealers Exchange, *Small Press Review,* and *Scavenger's Newsletter,* the "small press" enterprise is booming. More than ever before, big publishing houses are becoming less willing to gamble on unknown authors and non-mainstream works, sending good authors venturing out on their own.

Downsizing in big houses has reduced the number of editors available to work with new writers. Editors can spend less time with promising new authors, rejecting good work in favor of the proven saleable author. In addition to these drawbacks, large publishers seldom promote a book for more than six months after publication, moving on quickly to the next "sure thing."

To compound the problem for new authors, many agents are either refusing to offer editing services to make a book publishable, or are charging exorbitant reading and editing fees, sometimes exceeding $3,000. Unestablished authors can rarely afford such a subsidy.

These industry trends have left a conspicuous void in the publishing industry and provided a unique opportunity for independent publishers. More and more first-time and established authors are self-publishing their books—at handsome profits. While large publishers continue to offer only a 10% royalty on hard cover books, and a 7%–8% royalty on paperbacks, independent publishers realize a 25–100% profit on *each book* they sell. True, the advantages of being published by a "brand name" publisher are a huge print-run and instant national exposure. Self-publishing benefits can far outweigh these pluses by providing for a larger profit for as long as the author wishes to publish the book—oftentimes years. *Self-published books need never go out of print.*

Concise information-intensive paperback books of 48–248 pages, offered at a reasonable price, sell at consistently attractive profits throughout the United States and Canada. Eager and lucrative foreign markets in Australia, England, Germany, and Spain are opening up to American independently-published books.

Large Publishing House Policies and Requirements

Most large publishers want manuscripts from 60,000–80,000 words, though some will go as low as 40,000 or as high as 125,000 words. Word constraints are due to two factors: the cost of printing books, and the book buyers' perceptions of value (book thickness and quality) vs. price.

Format

Most publishers will accept book-length works in standard manuscript format only. This means letter-quality type in a mono-spaced font such as courier, double-spaced lines, 1 to 1½" margins all around, running headers with title and author name, and proper page numbering. Fancy type styles are unacceptable and must be denoted with <u>underline</u> for italics, squiggly lines for boldface.

Although some publishing houses will accept electronic submissions (by disk or modem), most still require a hard-copy manuscript in addition to electronic media.

Submissions Policies

Large publishers do not accept manuscripts without a first query; many also require a chapter-by-chapter synopsis of the book before submitting the manuscript. Some publishers would rather see a proposal (a book "plan") before you actually write the book. In many cases this is better for the author, as advances are often given for expenses incurred while writing—but not if the book is finished.

The biggest publishers will accept submissions through agents only; submissions through authors are not accepted. This includes Bantam/Doubleday, Simon and Schuster, Prentice-Hall, and Pocket Books.

Most publishers or agents require you to submit manuscripts by first-class mail with return postage provided. This can cost up to $10.00 each way ($20.00), not including photocopy costs (never send your original), and the cost of nested manuscript boxes.

Electronic Submissions

Electronic submissions follow different guidelines. The general rule is: the less formatting, the better. Use only one typeface and point-size, no double-spacing of lines required, italics are OK instead of underlining, hard returns only at the ends of paragraphs.

Agents

Most well-known agents are reluctant to accept unpublished authors. Many agents also charge a reading fee ($200.00 to $500.00); some charge materials and expenses fees ($75.00 to $200.00). In addition, some agents are now offering editing and rewriting services as extras, and charge up to $5,000.00 for these services. Lesser-known agents will sometimes waive reading and editing fees, but lesser-known agents have less clout with publishers than, say, the Scott Meredith Agency, New York's top literary agency.

Agents typically require a query, a chapter-by-chapter synopsis, and sample chapters of the book project before the author can submit a manuscript. This process can take from two to four months. Most agents get a standard 10%–20% royalty on the author's earnings—including advance—for domestic sales; 20%–25% on foreign sales. When an agent represents an author, the publisher sends the agent the advance and royalty checks, the agent takes out his/her percentage and then sends the author a check written on the agent's account. Be sure your agent is listed with one of the following agencies:

Society of Author's Representatives, Inc.
10 South Portland Avenue
Brooklyn, NY 11217

Independent Literary Agents Association, Inc.
432 Park Avenue South, Suite 1205
New York, NY 10016

Time and Money

It takes an average of two to three months to receive a reply to a query; two to six months after that for a reply to a solicited manuscript submission. Some publishers still frown upon simultaneous submissions.

Less than one-tenth of 1% of manuscripts submitted to publishers get accepted (that's less than one out of one thousand). It takes eight to twenty-four months after a publisher accepts a manuscript, for them to publish and release the book to the public; the average time is one year.

Most publishers offer an advance to authors. The average advance ranges from $200–$10,000 for an unknown, previously unpublished author, to millions for a bestselling author. Some large houses offer no advance at all. Advances are against earned royalties.

Royalty payments average 10% of the cover price of the hardcover edition of the book. A book that sells for $20.00 will earn the author $2.00 per copy—*after* deducting advances. Mass-market softcover books average a 7%–8% royalty: A softcover book that sells for $10.00 will earn the author 70–80 cents per copy. Publishers typically pay royalties quarterly or twice yearly, and not until the advance has been "earned back."

A recent trend in publishing is to pay a larger royalty on the *net profit*. While a 12–15% royalty may look good in a contract, when expenses—the cost of book printing and promotion—are deducted, it doesn't amount to much.

There is an old bromide in the publishing industry that states, "Even a bad book will sell 10,000 copies." Large publishing houses often order first print-runs of 2,000–5,000 copies for unknown authors, and increase print-runs cautiously as sales increase.

Books with a slow to average sales record will remain in print six to twelve months; best-sellers stay in print longer, sometimes—but rarely—years.

Editors

Editors have the right to change an author's work in any way deemed necessary to make the book attractive to readers and therefore profitable. First-time authors rarely have much say-so in this situation. Editors frequently change titles from the author's choice (*Gone With the Wind* was not Margaret Mitchell's title—she had originally named her famous book *Tomorrow is Another Day*). Publishers also do not require or desire the author's input on cover design: This is left to the design department of large houses.

Promotion

The publisher is responsible for ISBN assignment (see "ISBN" later in this chapter), promotion, marketing, and distribution of the book. Some publishers, however, require authors to attend book-signings at bookstores and schedule interviews on radio and TV talk shows to promote the book. What the publisher requires of the author varies greatly and will be outlined in the author's contract.

Contracts

Publishers buy the rights to publish and profit from your work. You still own the work and the copyright (see "Copyright" section later in this chapter), but not the rights to it until it may be released back to you by the publisher.

Do not copyright the material you send to publishers: A copyright notice on the title page is sufficient. The reason for this is that editors and publishers will inevitably alter your work, making the original copyright invalid for the published version. Publishers copyright your work for you *after* revisions.

Book contracts are typically from 25–60 pages long and contain legal terms, and many stipulations and conditions authors may not be prepared to handle. For this reason, most experts agree that an attorney should handle book contracts. There are lots of horror stories circulating that describe authors signing away all rights—including movie, audio cassette, and foreign rights—unknowingly. The author can essentially lose all future control of his/her work if he/she is not careful.

Once a book is out of print (the publisher drops it to concentrate energies and funds on more profitable works), the rights revert to the author and he/she can resubmit it to another house, or self-publish it.

Novelists may be interested to learn that series have more of a chance of being published than stand-alone novels. Editors and readers love a series based on familiar characters. Series sell very well, guaranteeing a market share for as long as the series runs—perhaps decades!

Recent trends indicate that a previously self-published book will have a better chance of being picked up by a large publisher than an unpublished manuscript. Sales records of the book will greatly influence this probability.

The Independent Publishing Option

Independent publishing can meet many of your publishing needs sooner than most big publishers. Depending on the complexity of the project, you can write, edit, typeset, design a cover for, and complete a first print-run of your book all within three to eight months.

Independent publishers operate in much the same way as large houses and will be responsible for copyright registration, ISBNs, promotion, and marketing. Many self-publishers enter into "cooperative" or "partnership" publishing in which several independent publishers share the expenses and marketing responsibilities.

Co-op publishing is not the same as publishing through a "vanity" press—in which all costs are paid by the author and marketing is also the author's responsibility—but it will require a substantial investment nevertheless. If you're going to subsidize publishing your book, you might as well do it all yourself and keep *all* of the profits.

Word counts for self-published and small-press books are more flexible: 10,000–word books are not unusual.

You can keep your book in print as long as you like. There are no CEOs to impress, no time limits on reaping the profits of sales.

You can update and revise your book, releasing a new edition every printing if you choose. This keeps the information up-to-date and the booksellers satisfied that you care about your book and your readers.

The title and cover design are up to you. If you don't have a design aptitude, professional designers can help you immeasurably, as they know what attracts people to a book, turning browsers into buyers.

Print-runs average 200–1,000 copies for most independent publishers (depending on funds). For high-quality perfect-bound books, lower print-runs make the per-copy cost high, but self-publishers can avoid excess inventory problems and remainders.

The book industry operates on some pretty strict standards: Books must be high quality, typeset professionally, UV-coated or laminated, bar-coded for bookstores to inventory easily, and have eye-catching covers. Bookstores buy attractive books on popular topics; the contents are secondary, but not altogether unimportant.

Profits, after expenses, are all yours. You will earn 25–100% on each book you sell, depending on the size of print-runs and method of distribution. On print-runs over 5,000 copies, your profit could increase to 300% on each book.

Generous discounts are an industry standard: Distributors ask for a 50–55% discount off the cover price; bookstores—40%; special-interest groups—25%; schools and libraries—20%.

You must price your books high enough to make a decent profit. (See "Pricing Strategy and Profit Calculation" in Part 11—Headache in a Can: Marketing.) Independently-published books are usually more expensive than mass-produced books, and this can be a deterrent to buyers...all the more reason to offer well-written, superior-quality books!

National media exposure can be slow unless distribution channels are wide open. Fortunately, many independent-press distributors are springing up all over the country as well as internationally, and are eager to work with independent publishers. Baker and Taylor, the world's largest distributor, has recently started accepting high-quality independently-published books. You will find a list of book distributors receptive to independently-published books in "Part 11—Headache in a Can: Marketing."

What Topics Sell?

Book topics can literally be anything that may interest another human. Obviously, the more humans you can interest, the more books you will sell. Anything for the general population has promise. How-to books are consistent best-sellers.

Large expensive books on hot topics will fare better than small books on less-popular topics.

Consistent Best-Sellers	Topics That Sell Poorly
nutrition, dieting, health	autobiographies
self-help	biographies
spirituality, new-age topics	personal essays
children's nonfiction	politics
children's story books	poetry
repair manuals	novels
computer books	
humor	
cookbooks	
attracting the opposite sex	
gambling	
investing	
get-rich-quick schemes	
marketing	
international commerce	
any how-to manual	

Book Planning

A great deal of careful planning goes into producing a book. The planning stage involves measuring, calculating, and brainstorming on paper.

Preliminaries:
Get it Right the First Time

Taking a raw manuscript to published book format is no simple task. The two formats are worlds apart, and many of the standards acceptable for one form are taboo for the other.

For those of you who are accomplished writers, you may safely skim over this chapter. If your writing skills could use some fine-tuning, settle in for a crash course in manuscript formatting and editing.

The Manuscript

It is best to type your book into a popular word processing program, such as Microsoft Word® or Corel WordPerfect®, and later import it into a page-layout program such as Adobe InDesign, PageMaker®, FrameMaker®, Serif PagePlus®, or Quark Xpress®. Word processors are easier to use than the text editors in page-layout programs, and they have many features text editors do not, such as irregular text-block selection, an on-line thesaurus, and footnote generators. Also, customize your word processor to show paragraph, tab, and space markers between words.

Manuscripts are usually formatted in the industry-standard manner that makes them easiest to read and edit. You will find standard manuscript format the best format for actually editing and rewriting your work. Standard format is as follows:

- Doubled-space the entire text.
- Use a monospaced font such as `courier` or `letter gothic`.
- Use 12-point type size.

- Set margins 1"–1½" all around—top, bottom, left, and right.
- Type your manuscript *flush left*. Do not justify your text—it leaves deceptive space between words that makes it harder to proofread for extra spaces that don't belong there.
- Type *two spaces* between sentences. This helps you see where one sentence ends and another begins. You will have to *globally replace* double-spaces with single spaces before importing the manuscript into a page-layout program for typesetting.
- Type only one space between colons and semicolons in compound sentences.
- Periods and commas go *inside* quotation marks—both double and single quotes.
- Denote "em" dashes with *two* hyphens; leave no space before or after them. (How many typists put a space, a hyphen, and a space to indicate em dashes? The problem is pandemic. It's wrong, and will add another error to the manuscript that you will have to correct before typesetting it.) InDesign will automatically replace double hyphens with bonafide typographer's em dashes when you import the manuscript into it.
- Underlining, usually indicating emphasis in a manuscript, is a no-no in typeset books. Use *italics* for emphasis—this is the final book format standard. If you underline instead of italicize, you'll have to globally replace all underlining with italics before importing the manuscript into a page-layout program.
- Standard manuscript format includes carriage returns at the ends of paragraphs, and after headings and subheadings. Keep in mind that extra returns will have to be stripped out (globally replaced with single returns) when preparing the manuscript for typesetting. In the page-layout program, we will use *white space* before and after headings instead of returns; it is more precise (allowing increments of hundredths of an inch) and when included in *styles* (explained in "Part

5—Banzai Typesetting"), ensures that spacing is consistent throughout your book.

Attempting to edit a manuscript that does not conform to the above standards will *double* your editing time. It is difficult to write notes and corrections on the printout if it isn't double-spaced. Extra spaces show up better if you use a monospaced rather than a proportional font, allowing you to swiftly remove rampant space-hiccups before typesetting.

Clear Writing

Clear writing is to a book what basting is to a Thanksgiving turkey. You can dress that turkey up with little white booties on the drumsticks and add sprigs of parsley, but if it's not cooked well, it's dog food. If your book is unnecessarily wordy, pretentious, and chock full of grammatical errors, clichés, and redundancies, it's fodder for the shredder. Superb design and layout will not redeem it. Pretty books make bad writing more apparent.

Starting Point

An outline is essential to planning and writing your book; it is a *road map* for clear writing. Microsoft Word for Windows has an outline feature that renumbers your outline automatically when you delete or insert entries. The most common and easiest to use outline is the standard format.

    I. CHAPTER 1
      A. Subhead
        1. second-level subhead
        2. second-level subhead
      B. Subhead
    II. CHAPTER 2
      A. Subhead
        1. second-level subhead
        2. second-level subhead
        3. second-level subhead
          a) third-level subhead
            (1) fourth-level subhead
              (a) fifth-level subhead
                (i.) sixth-level subhead
    III.   CHAPTER 3

Write a "stream-of-consciousness" first draft from your outline before you do anything else. Refrain from editing as you write—grammar, spelling, and punctuation are not important right now. Shove your personal critic in a dark closet and don't let the monster emerge until revision time. Revising and polishing come into consideration *after* your first draft. You will expend five to ten times more effort on revising than writing your first draft. Your first draft should be fun and unrestricted.

Structure and Format

Arrange your paragraphs in a logical sequence with smooth transitions. Choose one format and stick with it throughout your book: *general-to-specific* (introduction and then details—may include a summary), *specific-to-general* (details and then summary—may include an introduction), or *sequential/chronological* (recipes, assembly instructions, etc.).

Paragraph construction also follows a sequence. The first sentence introduces the paragraph. Succeeding sentences give details. The last sentence summarizes the paragraph and leads the reader into the next paragraph. Smooth transitions between paragraphs under a subheading create flow and provide a comfortable read.

> *Introduction*
> This is an interesting subject because it has so many facets and is important to many readers for many reasons, which I will describe.
> *Explain your subject*
> The first detail is this. The second detail is this other thing, and is rather involved. The third detail is the most interesting of all, so I've saved it till last to add impact.
> *Summary*
> Finally, all of these details together combine to make this an interesting subject. *(transition into next paragraph)* It is, however, associated with another interesting subject.
> *Introduction*
> This next subject will knock your socks off....

Let's Get Serious

It's time to appease the personal critic—you may now begin your revisions. How-to books need to be easy to read—this is your first concern. Your particular style of writing—your "authorial voice"—takes a back seat. Lock your ego behind bars and opt for clarity above everything else.

Clarity

Clarity means avoiding affected language, excessive jargon, puffery, vagueness, euphemism, and emotionally-charged words, as well as eliminating wordiness, redundancy, and cliché. Business and government often employ these very devices to make you react rather than think. *You* want to convey a concrete message. Your goal is to *express* rather than *impress*.

Affected language uses complex words instead of simple words.

Pretentious: The exquisite effulgence of the protagonist's malicious machinations are constructs the literary adjudicator will appreciate.

Translation: The critic will like the main character's cunning.

Affected Language	Common Language
adamantine	solid
adjudicate	judge
ascertain	find out
contiguous	joining
convoluted	complicated
elucidate	explain
expedite	hurry
ponderous	bulky
utilize	use

Affected language is essential in writing humor. Keep that in mind if you *don't* intend to be funny.

Vagueness is the enemy of clear writing—use concrete details rather than abstract concepts. Relative terms are vague. Words such as *some, few, less, more, rarely, occasionally, frequently, adequate, soon,* and *later* are relative terms—they relate (compare) to some (often unstated and therefore hazy) standard.

Vague: Books must have an *adequate* page count to bind them. They can then be displayed *properly* without taking up *too much* shelf space.

Concrete: Book page-count should be 32–500 pages so the spine will be wide enough for the title. The books can then be displayed spine out, taking up minimal shelf space.

Denotation and Connotation

Take care in choosing your words—they have a split personality. Words may *denote* something specific and concrete (the dictionary—*lexical*—definition) or *connote* something emotional and abstract. Strive to use *denotation* rather than *connotation* and readers will rarely misunderstand what you mean.

"Loaded" words are full of connotation. They contain subtle nuances and carry emotional baggage.

Connotation	Denotation
trash *(no one wants it)*	recyclables *(someone might want it)*
dude *(possibly a low-life)*	man *(a male human)*
stuff *(maybe trash...or not)*	things *(articles of possible value)*
smash *(destroy)*	compact *(fit in a smaller place)*

You will find connotation in street language:

"That dude over there ripped off my crap and then totally trashed my digs. I'm really bummed."

The above sentence is vague to those who don't know street lingo. Almost everyone will understand the translation:

"The man stole my belongings and then destroyed my house. I'm very upset."

You will often encounter puffery in advertising. Words such as *new, improved, fresh, natural, light, lavish, glamorous, exciting,* and *perfect* are common. These words mean nothing in themselves. *Light* relative to what?

Words such as *beautiful, ugly, normal, rich, poor, love, happiness, polluted, liberal, conservative,* and *peace* mean nothing in themselves. All of these words are relative to some obscure standard, some quantity that is never stated. They are emotionally charged and are meant to evoke feelings rather than thought.

Consider how the following words can have different connotations, depending on your values:

Evolution:	Change in the gene pool over time.
or...	Humans are descended from monkeys.
Catlike:	Sleek, graceful, and self-reliant.
or...	Sneaky, contrary, and territorial.
Liberal:	Open-minded, unhampered by orthodoxy or tradition, progressive.
or...	Bleeding-heart, egalitarian, wimp, pinko.
Abortion:	Termination of a process.
or...	Murder of an innocent being.
Vigilante:	Concerned citizen who takes action.
or...	Untrained terrorist who takes the law into his own hands.

Euphemism

Euphemism is at the heart of the politically-correct movement. Euphemism saps the life and real meaning from concepts in an attempt to *avoid* emotion. Euphemism clouds the issue and conceals responsibility by changing the *connotation* of an idea. This device is the refuge of government and medicine. The following are *real* and in common use:

EUPHEMISM	REAL MEANING
revenue enhancement	greed
negative economic growth	recession
therapeutic misadventure	physician-caused death
collateral damage	civilian deaths
eliminate with extreme prejudice	kill
incident	accident
error of omission	lie
withhold information	lie

EUPHEMISM	REAL MEANING
misdirect	lie
fails to meet functioning criteria	broken
nuclear exchange	dropping the bomb
decreased propensity for cell replication	aging
sudden deceleration	fall and impact
discomfort	pain
invasive procedure	surgery

As you can see, writers owe it to the reading public to avoid such contrived jargon. Tell the truth, keep it clear, and you'll succeed with your writing. I'll drink to that...uh, er...I resolve to responsibly imbibe sub-toxic amounts of ethanol (at home, nowhere near a motor vehicle) in honor of that statement....

Brevity

Use shorter sentences. Compound sentences (with clauses separated by commas) and complex sentences (with clauses separated by commas, semicolons, and colons) tend to distract readers, often forcing them to reread passages to get the full meaning. (Did you have to read that sentence over?) While complex constructions are sometimes necessary and add variety and interest to writing, paragraphs teeming with them are fatiguing to read. Conversely, paragraphs constructed of exclusively five-word sentences will read like a first-grade storybook and will destroy flow. Lack of flow irritates readers.

Complex Construction (avoid)

I have two days to finish this chapter, after which I will typeset it; I will then have accomplished my goal: a finished and polished book.

Choppy First-Grade Reader (avoid)

I will finish this chapter. It will take two days. I will then typeset it. I will then be finished with the book.

Good Sentence Variety (your goal)

I have two days to finish this chapter. I will then typeset it, finishing the book.

Use fewer words in favor of many. Long-winded sentences containing unnecessary words, redundancies, and clichés tax readers' patience and cloud the information.

Clutter

You can oftentimes eliminate single words such as *of*, *that*, *the*, and *then* without changing the meaning of the sentence.

Original:	Some *of the* writers at the conference *had to leave* early. *If they had stayed, then* they would have enjoyed the lecture by David Brin. (25 words)
Rewritten:	Some writers at the conference left early. They would have enjoyed David Brin's lecture. (14 words)

Cut clutter by eliminating trite phrases that serve no purpose (corrections in parentheses):

- must be accomplished by (by)
- in order to (to)
- it has been shown that *(eliminate!)*
- please do not hesitate to (please)
- is dependent on (depends on)
- in spite of the fact that (despite)
- by using (use)

Redundancy

When you state something twice (or more) in different ways, it is redundant. Redundancies are inane, superfluous, and pointless. Some common ones:

- square in shape (square *is* a shape)
- red in color (red *is* a color)
- eleven AM in the morning (AM *is* morning)
- very necessary (*very* implies *more than*)
- few in number (few refers to a relative *number*)
- totally destroyed (as opposed to *partial* destruction? That's only damage.)
- truly precise (nothing can be *more than* precise)
- famous celebrity (celebrity *means* famous)

Cliché

If you've heard it once, you've heard it a thousand times: Clichés are overused sentence fragments and common sayings that clutter writing. Some not-so-obvious clichés often sneak into good writing:

- during the course of (during)
- in the vast majority of cases *(eliminate!)*
- at this point in time (now)
- on a monthly basis (monthly)
- until such time as (when, until)
- due to the fact that (because)

The Active Voice

Personalize your prose. Speak to your reader. Use the word *you*, *I*, or *we*, or an implied *you*.

Impersonal:	The book was typeset using InDesign, and then output on a high-quality printer.
Personalized:	I typeset the book using InDesign, then I printed it.
Direct Address:	(you) Typeset the book using InDesign; then (you) print it.

Personalizing writing automatically means making it active. Passive references are history—we don't write like that anymore. Avoid *to be* constructions such as *is, was, are, am, being, been,* and *were.* Things don't mysteriously happen by themselves anymore—now actors *do* things to something.

Passive:	The bound books *were* put on the lift and then trimmed. Next, the books *will be* shipped to the warehouse. (no actors)
Active:	The pressman *put* the books on the lift and *trimmed* them. He then *shipped* them to the warehouse. (actor *doing*)

Suppressed verbs leech the power from writing and muddy its meaning. Words ending in *-ing, -tion, -ancy, -ance, -ment,* and *-ent* indicate suppressed verbs.

Suppressed:	*Completion* of the printing process has been accomplished by the pressman. *Binding* must now be done.
Active:	The pressman has *completed* the printing. He will now *bind* the books.

Involve the reader with active verbs and you have him or her hooked for the duration of your book. But, there are times when passive, impersonal sentences simply read better than active, personal ones. Choose active verbs when they work—no need to force a perfectly good passive sentence into active form.

Unintentional Comedy

Watch for misplaced modifiers. Misplaced modifiers can transform highly effective prose into farce. There are only three constructions you need to worry about: dangling participles, split infinitives, and gerunds.

Dangling Participle

Nothing can lend more hilarity to a sentence than a dangling participle:

> *The writer found a pencil walking to the mailbox.*
> Pencils do not walk—rewrite:
> - *The writer found a pencil while walking to the mailbox.* (This is the simplest form.)
> - *While walking to the mailbox, the writer found a pencil.* (This is a compound sentence—it has a comma separating two clauses.)
> - *The writer, while walking to the mailbox, found a pencil.* (This form is more complex than the other two because it has two commas.)

Split Infinitive

When an adverb precedes a verb, you have a split infinitive.

> - The self-publisher *quickly exited* through the door before the agent spotted him.
> The form should read, "...exited quickly..."

Gerund

If you've ever seen a noun used as a verb, you've just spotted the woolly-chested gerund. It will never be on the endangered species list, as it is in a successful captive breeding program. We'll have lots more as time grinds on. Examples are *partying, rapping, servicing,* and *testing.* Some gerunds are valid *(testing)* while others are associated with street lingo *(rapping).* The suffix *-ize* also flags a gerund. Politicians like to *familiarize, formalize,* and *finalize* a lot. Verbing nouns is a prerequisite in politics.

Negative—*Not!*

Avoid negative construction where appropriate. This means using positive, active verbs rather than negative words that sound like reprimands or ultimatums (unless you need to scare readers). Negative constructions make readers *feel* rather than understand.

Negative:	*Do not* use slang and street lingo in your how-to book (unless it's *about* street lingo). You risk *not being* understood and your self-publishing enterprise *may not* succeed.
Positive:	*Avoid* using slang in your book, unless your book is *about* slang. You risk *alienating* your audience, and your self-publishing enterprise may *fail.*

Editing and Revising

Editing your manuscript entails reading it several times clear through from hardcopy. It is a curious thing, but catching all errors on the screen is nearly impossible. No one knows whether this is due to eye fatigue or familiarity, but I guarantee you'll miss some of the most obvious bloopers on screen; they'll jump right out and slap you in the face from paper printout.

It is not unusual for a manuscript or final book proof to go through ten to twenty revisions. In fact, ten to twenty is fairly standard. (Some writers put their manuscripts through dozens of revisions. If they are not initially in need of psychological counseling, they will be by the hundredth revision.)

Even with twenty revisions, you will become so sick of your book, you will crave to sacrifice it to RAMulus and ROMulus—the computer gods who transform coherent binary code into hash. Before this happens, enlist the help of an experienced friend to catch what you will inevitably miss. Outside help in editing and proofreading is your only redemption from being reduced to a drooling, shuffling cretin.

Compositors (typesetters) hate messy over-edited manuscripts from which to typeset a book. This is referred to as *penalty copy*. It's punishment for the compositor, so the compositor is glad to pass the misery on to you in increased charges. Now that you're doing it all yourself, you'll be careful to avoid too much hand-editing. Train yourself to edit on the computer as much as possible so that your final printout is clean.

In large publishing houses, the designer makes notes on the original manuscript called *markups*. The manuscript may also include *roughs*—crude sketches indicating where artwork will be placed in the manuscript. Use these techniques on your manuscript; they will help you plan and typeset your book.

Misused Words

Never underestimate the power and clarity of good grammar. Many word processors have grammar checkers in them that can be modified to scrutinize your writing for violations of every known law of good writing, or they can be set to skip over some rules so your writing has a more friendly and laid-back style.

Though rules for good writing are somewhat more relaxed than in grade-school days, several bloopers seem ubiquitous in today's media.

For those of us who aspire to excellence and lucidity, we'll need to watch for these misused words:

1. *Which* used interchangeably with *that:*

    Which gives additional information about the subject, and is set off with a comma. It is parenthetical in nature. "I will typeset my book today, *which* I finished editing yesterday."

    That identifies what's being referred to and has no comma after it. "This is the book *that* I will typeset today."

2. Confusion between *its* and *it's:*

    Its is a possessive reference. "*Its* pages appear crowded."

    It's always means *it is*. "*It's* the tight leading that's causing the pages to appear crowded."

3. *Further* confused with *farther:*

    Further refers to amount or additional time. "We must read *further* about good grammar."

    Farther denotes distance only. "How much *farther* is the bookstore?"

4. Confusion of *affect* and *effect:*

    Affect means to have an influence. "The poem *affect*ed me deeply."

    Effect means to cause an outcome or produce a result. "I don't expect some sappy poem to *effect* any changes in my life. Unless there are unknown side-*effect*s."

5. Use of *like* instead of *as, that, such as,* or *as if:*

    Like means similar to or indicates how someone feels; it is comparative and emotive. "This book is *like* no other. I feel *like* dancing."

    That is also emotive. "I feel *that* writing this book was hard work."

    As refers to something. "*As* I said before, watch out for the misuse of *like.*"

    Such as refers to an example to follow. "There are useless examples, *such as* these: 1, 2, 3, 4."

    As if denotes a hypothetical situation. "I write this book *as if* it will actually help someone."

6. *Comprise* and *compose* used interchangeably:

    The whole *comprises* the parts. "The book *comprises* several pages."

    The parts *compose* the whole. "The pages *compose* the book."

7. Use of *could of* instead of *could have:*

    There is no such phrase as *could of*. The use of *could of* probably stems from the fact that *could have* is often spoken as the contraction *could've*. "You *could have* guessed that."

8. Confusion of *lay* and *lie:*

    Lay means to place something down. *Lay* requires a thing. "*Lay* this book down for awhile before you strain your gray matter." The past tense of lay is *laid*. "Go back to where you *laid* that book down."

    Lie means to recline or situate yourself in a recumbent position. "After you lay that book down, go *lie* down with your suspicious cat."

The past tense of *lie* is *lay*. "It was warm and cozy where you and your cat *lay* together."

9. Confusion between *whose* and *who's*:

Whose indicates ownership; it is a possessive term. "*Whose* advice shall I take on grammar?"

Who's is the contraction of *who is*. "*Who's* the most knowledgeable person to consult on grammar?"

10. Use of *try and* in place of *try to*:

"Americans must always *try to* polish their grammar; never *try and* polish it, unless you are British writing for a British audience."

11. Confusion of *can* and *may*:

Can denotes ability. "You *can* read this book, because you know how to read."

May indicates permission or possibility. "You *may* read this book if you can afford to buy it. You *may* buy it if you like it."

12. Use of *imply* and *infer* interchangeably:

Imply means to state indirectly. "Do you mean to *imply* that I don't know what I'm talking about?"

Infer means to draw a conclusion. "You may *infer* from the evidence at hand, that I know of what I speak."

13. Confusion of *fewer* and *less*:

Fewer refers to separate things that can be counted. "*Fewer* people read today than have read in decades past."

Less indicates a collective or things that cannot be counted as separate. "I have *less* guts than some people do when defragmenting their hard drives." An exception to the rule is time and money: "I have *less* than two months to complete this book." "I made *less* money last year than I expect to make this year; however, I will have *fewer* dollars left in my hand this year due to increased taxes."

14. Misuse of *good* and *well*:

Good describes a sensation. "It feels *good* to be able to write uninterrupted."

Well is a value judgment. "I write *well* when I am left undisturbed."

15. Misuse of *bad* and *badly*:

Bad describes sensations. "When my computer is down, I feel *bad*."

Badly is a value judgment. "I type *badly*; thank goodness for spelling-checkers."

16. Confusion of *between* and *among*:

Between always compares two things. "*Between* you and I, book production is going to be one hell of a ride." "What is the difference *between* traditional publishing and self-publishing?"

Among compares more than two things. "*Among* those who publish their own books, the extraordinary effort and hairpulling entailed is understood as a given." "Self-publishers must choose *among* several publishing options."

17. Use of *different than* rather than *different from*:

Things cannot be *different than* other things.

Things can only be *different from* other things. That is, they *differ from* them; they cannot *differ than* them.

18. Confusion of *use to* and *used to*:

There is no such phrase as *use to*; *use* implies utility, function.

Used to indicates what was, what has been. "Books *used to* be typeset with metal letters."

19. Phrases such as *I wish I was*...instead of *I wish I were*, or, *if I was you*, instead of *if I were you*...:

I wish I was is an incorrect form of *I wish I were*. The statement is hypothetical—it has happened only in your imagination, and so *were* is used instead of *was*. "*I wish I were* smart enough to tell you precisely why. *If I were you*, I'd just accept the rule at face value and not belabor the point."

20. Verbs that don't agree in number with their subjects:

"Or, *verbs that don't agree in number with its subjects*." Argh.

21. Pronouns that don't agree in number with their antecedents:

"*Everyone* who writes must discipline *themselves* to succeed at it." *Everyone* is singular; *themselves* is plural. It is better to rewrite this sentence: "*Writers* must discipline *themselves* to succeed at it (but every*one* has *one's* own opinion on this)."

The misuse of *we* and *us*, and *he* and *him* (or *she* and *her*) is also common. "*We* three went to the publisher's convention (*us* didn't go to the convention)." "They four took *us* to the publisher's convention (they didn't take *we* to the convention).” “It was *he* who invited us (*him* didn't invite us).”

22. Use of double negatives:

   I can't get no satisfaction logically breaks down into *I want dissatisfaction, and I cannot get it.* All I get is satisfaction—there is no absence of it anywhere. So what are you moaning about, Mick?

23. Use of nonexistent words abounds. There are no such words as *alot* (a lot), *alright* (all right), *analyzation* (analyze), *irregardless* (regardless), and *metabolization* (metabolism or metabolize). *Awhile* used to be two words; it is now one denoting a nonspecific short time.

In addition to being vigilant in tracking down grammatical brain-burps, assess your manuscript for readability with a computerized grammar checker. It may surprise you to know that the general reader comprehends written work at about the sixth- to seventh-grade level. A reading level much past eighth grade is appropriate for an undergraduate text and technical manuals, but you will lose general readers if that is your target audience.

Grammar checkers may include a readability assessment that calculates reading ease, grade level (both of the *Flesch* scale), and something called a *Gunning Fog Index.*

Standard writing averages 15 words per sentence, 145 syllables per 100 words, is grade level 7–8, and has a low “fog” index. Readability statistics are a comparison of *your* writing to standard writing. A word processor calculates these statistics through the average number of sentences per paragraph, words per sentence, number of syllables per 100 words, and number of characters per word.

The Gunning Fog Index rates your writing for sentence length and the number of words per sentence more than a syllable long. Multisyllabic sentences are harder to read (such as this one). The lower the fog index number, the easier the material is to read. Ideally, your writing should be comfortable to read aloud—that is the true acid test. If your tongue wanders around looking for places to do push-ups in your mouth, your writing is too complicated.

READING EASE	FLESCH SCORE	FLESH GRADE LEVEL
very easy	90–100	4
easy	80–90	5
moderately easy	70–80	6
standard	60–70	7
moderately difficult	50–60	9–10
difficult	30–50	11–14*
very difficult	0–30	15–20*

The Gunning Fog Index ranges from 0 to 100. A score below 10 can be read aloud by a winded, stuttering, asthmatic, senior citizen.

Punctuation

Improper punctuation can make happy perfectionists mutate into anal-retentive obsessive-compulsive ghouls. There is no excuse for screwing up punctuation—there's not much of it and it's not hard to remember.

- *Periods* come at the ends of sentences. When quotes come at the end of a sentence, the period goes *inside* the quotes. *Always.*

- *Commas* come after clauses—or more intuitively—commas should be placed where it would be natural to pause briefly while reading the sentence out loud.

  Most importantly, commas keep the meaning of a sentence perfectly clear. How would you read: “It's all over my friend”? Is the relationship or event finished, or is your friend covered in some hideous substance? Consider, “It's all over, my friend.” Adding a comma leaves no doubt as to meaning.

  Commas are the most misused punctuation; either the manuscript is peppered with them in unnecessary places, or there is such a paucity of commas that the sentences run on in one breathless sweep. Commas occur *inside* double or single quotes. Improper use of commas will identify your work as amateurish.

- *Dashes*—more accurately referred to as *em* dashes because they theoretically occupy the same space as a capital *M* in typesetting—are used to set off a parenthetical phrase, such as the one in this sentence. Dashes are also used to indicate a longer pause than a comma would, or an abrupt stop if used at the end of a sentence.

- *Ellipses* dots (three dots separated by non-breaking spaces, or generated with the ASCII code

[Alt] [0][1][3][3] for DOS-based machines, and [Alt] [;] on the Mac) are used to indicate a very long pause...or to denote omitted text, especially in a direct quote or long passage from another written work. A final ellipses at the end of a sentence occurs after a period—so it appears as four dots.

- *Colons* are used to separate an introductory sentence from an example or list that follows. "For example: This sentence follows as an example of the first part of this sentence." "For example: item 1, item, 2, item 3." When the material following the colon is complete (not missing a subject or verb), the first letter is capitalized. When it is incomplete, the first letter of the clause following the colon is *not* capitalized.

- *Semicolons* separate clauses in which the second clause modifies or refers back to the first clause. "Books are meant to be read; they are also meant to be treasured; however, engaging in the latter but not the former is characteristic of a collector, not a reader."

- *Double-Quotes* indicate spoken dialog, words used as words (though italics are better for this), and metaphorical phrases that may have nonstandard connotations associated with them when used within a certain context. In the latter case, a person may be a "dog," but a dog is just a dog.

  In dialog that runs longer than one paragraph, ending quotes go on the last paragraph *only*.

- *Single-Quotes* indicate quotes within quotes. I said, "There is more than one way to skin a cat when it comes to book production. But Myrtle said, 'You're not only cruel to felines, but everybody knows there is only one way to do anything, and book making is no exception.'" So much for Myrtle's creativity, not to mention her grasp of clichés.

- The use of **Question Marks** and *Exclamation Points* is pretty obvious, but where to place them relative to quotes may not be. If the question mark or exclamation mark is part of the phrase in quotations, put this punctuation *inside* the quotes. If it is not part of the quoted material but is associated with the originating sentence, put it *outside* the quotes. I told Judy how many words were in this book and she said, "Holy cow!" How does one respond to a phrase like "Holy cow"?

  It is tacky and childish to use more than one exclamation point or question mark after a sentence. Advertising copy is an exception.

- *Apostrophes* indicate possession and are used to replace missing letters in a contraction. An apostrophe before the *s* denotes ownership by an individual; after the *s*, by a group. "Don Egbert's IQ is abysmal. The Egberts' IQs are abysmal."

  "I can't explain this any better." (The apostrophe in *can't* replaces the *o* and *n* in the word *cannot*.)

- *Hyphenated phrases* are useful when the meaning of a collection of words could be misconstrued. Consider this phrase: DIGITAL MACHINE CLEANING INSTRUCTIONS. Without hyphens in strategic places, we don't know whether the instructions are digital (as in computerized) or the cleaning instructions are for digital machines. If the latter, then the phrase should read DIGITAL-MACHINE CLEANING INSTRUCTIONS.

  Hyphens are also needed for a string of words representing an entire thought: "Know-it-alls make me nauseous. *Know-it-alls* is a complete thought representing a much-maligned sector of the population.

  Use hyphens at the ends of words that share words in common with other hyphenated words, as in *minority- and women-owned business*, or *upper- and lowercase*. This convention is more readable than *minority-owned and women-owned business*, or *uppercase and lowercase*.

- *Abbreviations* in the body of your book look tacky, unless they are acronyms for famous organizations or brands of merchandise (NATO, IBM). Avoid abbreviating street (st.), foot (ft.), or pounds (lbs.). These abbreviations are acceptable in tables.

Finally, some literary irritations serve only to clutter and confuse writing:

- The use of *so, therefore* together in a concluding statement is redundant—*so* and *therefore* mean the same thing.

- The use of *frequently* and *often* as different words—they mean the same thing. One is not a degree more or less than the other.

- Too many *the*s—it makes your book look like a Dick-and-Jane reader.

- Too many *that*s. You can often delete this word without detracting from the meaning of the sentence.

- The use of *then* following an *if* clause. If you write clearly, you will not need *then* after the comma.

- Writing *can not*, when *cannot* has been a single word for decades.

- Using prepositions such as *where* and *over* in places they don't belong. *Where* is a place; over is a *position*. *Wrong:* "This is the car *where* the oil is leaking." *Right:* "This is the car *in which* the oil is leaking." *Wrong:* "There was confusion *over* the two books" (not unless you're hovering in the air or standing on them). *Right:* "There was confusion *between* the two books" (though *between* signifies position, it also denotes distinction).

Word Count

When creating and putting together a book, it is best to save each chapter or section as a separate file; they are easier to handle, and should gremlins attack, your whole book won't be corrupted, only the chapter file in which the error occurred. The problem with books split into several files is that it's hard to get a word count unless you like to add columns of numbers. Why is a word count important? It's the most accurate way to estimate how many final book pages you will have—and whether you should cut or pad-out the page count to fit the number and kind of signatures you'll be setting up for your book.

Microsoft Word has a nifty cheater's shortcut that will allow you to count all the words across several files. By chaining chapter files in a *master document*, you can get a total word count.

Before employing this shortcut, you must be sure to check the *Show: field codes* box under OPTIONS at the bottom of the TOOLS menu. (When you choose OPTIONS, choose the VIEW tab.)

The following instructions may vary slightly with different versions of Microsoft Word, but the general principles are the same. Start a new document and choose FIELD from the INSERT menu. In the FIELD NAMES, choose INCLUDE TEXT, and type in the name of the book chapter—with file extension—in the FILENAME: box. Do this until all of the chapters are listed in a neat column in your master document. Each chapter will be enclosed in brackets {}, which tells the computer that there's stuff associated with this field—in this case, an entire chapter is stored in the field code—you just can't see it. If the FIELD CODES box is not checked in OPTIONS: VIEW from the TOOLS menu, when you insert the field, your entire chapter will show up. If you keep doing this, the whole book will rewrite itself and your computer may run out of memory.

After you've assembled the *master.doc*, go to PROPERTIES under the FILE menu and click the STATISTICS tab. Word will do a word count for the entire book. If you save the *master.doc*, keep in mind that this one page contains all the data for all of the chapters, and will take up as much disk space as the separate chapter files combined. It's like having two copies of your book on the disk. It's up to you whether you have the space on your hard drive to do this.

If you modify any of your chapters after making a master document, you can update the field codes by highlighting them, then pressing the F9 function key.

Book Size, Page Count, and Dimensions

Estimating the total pages a book will have is known as *casting off* the book. Knowing the total word count of your book will help you cast off the book.

Books that aren't thick enough to justify their projected cover price are sometimes *padded-out* by adding white space, increasing the margins, type size and leading, and adding "fluff" (unnecessary wordage) to increase the page count.

Books that are too long cost more to produce and reap fewer profits. You can reduce page count by changing fonts, and by reducing type size, leading, margins, and white space. This must be done with care (described later) to prevent pages from looking crowded.

Generally, 1–1½ manuscript pages will make one 5½" x 8½" book page. This may vary according to margin width, font and point-size used, leading, and white space. All of these elements will be described as we go along.

Big Publishers' Method of Calculating Projected Book Size from Manuscript Length

Manuscript Specs:
  8½" by 11"
  1½" margins all around
  24 double-spaced lines per page
  Characters per page at 10 cpi (pica) = 1320
  Characters per page at 12 cpi (elite) = 1584

Book Characters per Page (standard trim size)

	6⅛" x 9½"	7⅜" x 9¼"	8" x 10"
1 column	3,200	3,500	3,800
2 columns	—	3,800	4,800
Part Openers:	2 printed pages		
Chapter Openers:	1 printed page		

Illustrations:
  ⅓ page (1-column books);
  ¾ page (2-column books)

Front and Back Matter:
  16–48 pages per book

Calculations—Example
  Printed Book Pages:.....................................250
  Trim Size:...6" x 9"
  Columns/page:...1

Deduct:
  Part Openers:...-10
  Chapter Openers:.......................................-21
  Front and Back Matter:................................-16
  Illustrations:..- 6
  (⅓ page each x 18 illustrations)

Total Deductions:...-53
  Book pages minus deductions:...................197
  Dividing characters per book page:..........3,200
  ...by characters per manuscript page:......1,320
  ...results in a factor of:.............................2.4

Multiply factor (2.4) times book pages:
  478 Manuscript Pages = 250 Finished Book Pages

These calculations are accurate only if you typeset your books exactly as the Big Guys do. Look at some of their books and decide for yourself.

In general, 5½" x 8½" self-published books from 48–248 pages sell the easiest. They are also the easiest to prepare for press and the least expensive to print. Small books can be written and sold fairly quickly. Books smaller than 64 pages are regarded as booklets or pamphlets and can rarely be bound attractively. Most booklets are *saddle-stitched* (stapled through the middle) and are best sold through direct mail at low cost to unwary buyers.

Large-sized (8½" x 11") books and books with higher page counts sell less successfully because they are more expensive to print and must therefore have a fairly high cover price. It's not easy for buyers to part with $39.95 for a softcover book. Think twice before considering publishing an expensive book.

Adhering to a Schedule

To successfully market your own books, you will have to adhere to a production schedule. The schedule allows you to estimate and coordinate your activities so you can get your books out into the marketplace when distributors and bookstores expect them.

The time from presentation of a raw manuscript to typesetting the book into galleys is called the *turnaround time*. This is the time when things can get quite hairy—mostly because at this point more things can go wrong. Once the book is ready to go to press, you will lose all control of time schedules because you'll be operating on the printer's and the binder's schedules.

The time between the projected publication date and the finished bound book is called the *lead time*. Sufficient lead time makes life worth living. When you register your books with national databases, you have to tell the registering agencies an estimated publication date, and then do your damnedest to meet that deadline. Don't underestimate how much time you'll need—you'll be starkly surprised.

Should you find yourself unable to meet projected release dates, expect to experience much growling from distributors via tracer forms. Apologize immediately and profusely, and state a new release date you *know* you can meet.

Large-House Book Production Schedule

Total Weeks	Tasks to be Completed
6–8	transmittal, copyediting, author review; designer prepares layout
1	designer marks copyedited manuscript
3	typesetting
3	proofreading galleys (first-pass proofs)
2	typeset corrections and create page proofs
2	proofread page proofs; indexing
1.5	typeset corrections, make repro-proofs
1.5	check and correct repro-proofs
6–8	camera work, bluelines, printing, binding
1	ship books to warehouse from bindery
2–4	ship books to distributors and bookstores
29–35	total weeks required to make a book

Independent publishers can realistically cut this time by 30–50%. Fewer people in the chain of command translates to increased efficiency and quick turnaround.

Book Registration

To convince book buyers you're serious, your books must be copyrighted, registered with an International Standard Book Number (ISBN), and perhaps placed in the Library of Congress.

The Ins and Outs of Copyrights

Creative expression is one of our most human of attributes. Copyright law governs the creative expression of intellectual property, ranging from visual arts such as paintings, sketches, architectural design, photographs, and motion pictures; to performance arts, such as dance choreography, comedy sketches, dramatic vignettes, and music performance; to digital creations such as software programming, on-line text, electronically designed posters, and web graphics. No matter what type of business in which you engage, your lives will inevitably be touched by issues of copyright.

As a self-publisher, you will be responsible for registering your own copyrights.

The Concept/Expression Dichotomy

Copyright, in its most basic sense, protects *creative expression* only. It does not protect *ideas*. To the extent that you may copy someone's concept, but not the *expression* of that concept, you are generally safe from copyright infringement. (This may not, however, apply to trademarks—another issue altogether, and beyond the scope of this book.) All creative work is protected the moment it is produced in tangible form, and copyright registration need not be officially filed to claim copyright. However, recovery of some court fees and winning a copyright infringement action may depend upon official validation with copyright registration.

Small portions of copyrighted work may be used under restricted circumstances, constituting "fair use." It is permissible to use limited portions of a work for quotes, and for purposes such as commentary, criticism, news reporting, and scholarly papers.

Intellectual property that has *not* been committed to tangible form, i.e., a song or choreography, an improvisation or other performance that remains in the creator's head, cannot be copyrighted until it is consigned to tangible form. If you don't write down that clever joke you just made up, anyone who does so, can claim to own it and use it however they want.

The Thin Gray Line

Sometimes it is not all that easy to distinguish between concept and expression. Case in point: Apple vs. Microsoft in the issue of the GUI (graphical user interface) in computer operating systems. This case was in court a long time while prominent thinkers toiled over fair use, and whether a GUI was a concept or an expression of a concept. Similar cases arrive in court every day, and the experts may still find such distinctions difficult.

To qualify as protectable expression, the creation must exhibit some sort of originality. The creator of a work has the exclusive right to display, reproduce, distribute, and offer for sale the work, as well as any derivative work. Generally speaking, a derivative work must be unrecognizable to the creator of the original to be free of copyright infringement, but this is a gray area in the courts. The experts are divided as to how much change is required before a derivative work can stand as an original creative expression of a concept. Generally, if the original artist recognizes it as hers or his, there will most probably be trouble.

Copyright Duration

The duration of copyright is currently the creator's life plus 70 years. Copyrights that expire after this time become part of the public domain, unless the copyright is renewed by heirs or is assigned to a new owner to which copyright has legally been transferred. Copyrights may be transferred to your heirs through your will, and again through their wills—for generations if the copyright is continually renewed. Works in the public domain may be used or altered freely by others. Be sure to cite and to thank (or apologize to) the original artist for inspiration for a derivative work of public-domain property.

Copyright Parameters

Copyright covers five basic areas in which rights can be collectively or individually assigned. When you submit work to someone else for a specific purpose, it is essential that both parties understand what rights and any inclusions/exclusions, are being negotiated. Your rights as a copyright owner extend to five areas:

- **Display Rights**—involve the public display or transmission of the work;
- **Performance Rights**—cover the rights to perform the work in public (as in dance, music, or movies);
- **Distribution Rights**—encompass the sale and profit from the work (many be monetary, or in the case of free distribution, the benefit of exposure of your creativity to the public);
- **Reproduction Rights**—embrace the creation of copies or substantially similar copies of the work;
- **Derivation or Adaptation Rights**—embody creation of work derived or adapted from another work.

By law, copyrights include all of the five rights even if not stated in a contract. You may selectively assign one or more of your rights in a contract, or exclude certain rights for any particular work. You may request and purchase from another, one or more of these rights to their work, while excluding the other rights. For example, publishers may contract with authors for exclusive electronic publishing rights, which permits the author to seek a different publisher for trade text publishing opportunities. Movie producers may buy rights to a script, while the same script can be sold to a book publisher at the same time for paperback adaptation.

One exception to creator-as-owner of the copyright, is when a creative work is within the scope of employment by an employee for an employer. Such work is considered *work for hire,* and the artist, writer, or other creator does not own the work—the employer does. This is generally understood within the American workplace, and is rarely negotiable. This principle may also apply to commissioned work, such as artwork or ghostwriting. Be

especially careful regarding work-for-hire creations if you wish to retain copyright. For commissioned work, your contract needs to elucidate your terms very specifically.

Derivative Works

It is also important to understand that there is a substantial difference between the actual work of art, and the *copyright* of that art. For example, purchasing a painting makes you the owner of the painting, but not the owner of the copyright of that painting. You may not, without express written permission of the artist, make greeting cards from that painting, as this constitutes a derivative work and the creator retains these copyrights, not you. For you to legally make greeting cards, calendars, labels, or other items from the original art, the artist must assign and release these rights to you in a written contract.

What Constitutes Creative Work?

Literary Works

Most people are aware that copying a written work and presenting it as their own—even from an advertising piece or the World Wide Web—is copyright infringement. We learned the meaning of *plagiarism* in school, and perhaps witnessed with secret delectation, an unlucky few get caught doing it. While *topics* cannot be copyrighted (nor can article, book, song, play, or film titles), the manner in which the theme is *presented,* most certainly can. Use care in extracting copy from preprinted articles and book chapters. If the subject is simply irresistible to you, write the article yourself in your own words. Then...*rewrite, rewrite, rewrite!* Your finished work should bare no resemblance whatsoever to the original work. (We used to employ the rule-of-thumb that no five words in succession must resemble the original. This is an oversimplification, and may still put you at risk for copyright infringement.)

Written work submitted to periodicals is typically handled in a manner peculiar to periodicals. When you submit your article, you automatically give that periodical First North American Serial Rights, which means that it may be used only once in the periodical to which you submit it. This policy does not have to be stipulated anywhere; it's industry-standard. If the publisher then wishes to use your article in, say, an additional month's issue, a yearly "best of" edition, or in another anthology, the publisher must then request such rights from the author. In addition, authors may not use the *rewritten and published version* of their work in another publication; author copyrights are confined to their *original* work only (otherwise, it would be like getting a free rewrite). If your work has been substantially rewritten after submission to a periodical (an extreme rarity, as rejection is more likely if rewriting is actually required), you must request permission to use that version elsewhere, or to have rights to this *new version* completely revert back to you.

Recipes

In general, a list of ingredients for a recipe is not copyrightable. Only the preparation instructions—if original and unique—will get that fabulous recipe copyrighted and protected against duplication.

Illustration, Graphic, and Web Design

Many graphic designers and illustrators conduct their business in accordance with guidelines developed by the *Graphic Artists Guild* and the *Electronic Design Association*. These guidelines encourage the artist to assign rights individually and specifically in a contract. Otherwise, graphic artists may be shocked to discover that the logo they were hired to design for a flyer, appears on the business web-site, stationery, business cards, envelopes, and all manner of documents the original artist never designed. The graphic artist, in such a case, has the right to sue for copyright infringement and collect damages. Graphic artists and illustrators are also encouraged to retain ownership and possession of all *source documents* for their designs, transferring to the client only the finished, commissioned art (a practice common to photographers, in retaining negatives). Artists may, of course, at their own discretion, develop their own policies regarding source documents, as long as they outline these policies in a contract. *In lieu of a contract, however, all five copyright parameters are considered in force automatically.*

Music—Live and Recorded

Most of us are aware that it is illegal to copy a music CD or tape, and transfer it to another person—either for free or for profit. In either case, the original artist gets cheated of royalties for this copyright infringement. Copyrights also apply to live musical performances. For example, some musicians openly forbid audience taping of a live performance. This policy is not only part of a musician's copyrights at the creation of the work, it may even be part of their recording contract with a music publishing company.

Performance Art—Dance Choreography, Acting Scripts, and Comedy Routines

Dancers and other performance artists may be interested in protecting their choreography or scripts so that other performers may not duplicate their movements or dialog in other performances without their permission. In cases of unique and original choreography or scripts, it may be wise for artists to inquire as to whether their performances will be videotaped as part of "the show." If a performer is aware an event in which he or she appears is going to be taped, he or she then gives *implied consent* to also being taped as part of that event, *unless restrictions are outlined in a separate written contract*. Some videographers and photographers are alert to possible artist objections over recording their appearances, and may ask performers to sign artist or model release forms. There is no shame in getting everything down in writing; it helps assuage any conflicts that may ensue due to misunderstanding, and makes for a more confident working environment.

Software, Fonts, and Clip Art

Most computer users are all too aware of the copyright laws regarding software piracy (why, thank you, Microsoft). Most software users understand that they purchased a *license* to use the software, and that they do not own the software outright. But, did you know that simply giving someone a font so that they can create your brochure for you, or innocently handing over clip art to another, may also violate copyright laws? Most clip art for sale is not only copyrighted, but the specific rights of use are frequently outlined either in a *readme* document on the CD, or on the CD jacket itself. Such conditions frequently state that you have a *license* to use the clip art, and such use is royalty-free—you don't have to pay the artist anything to use it—but only for the original purchaser of the CD, not for anyone else. Some clip art has other use restrictions on it: no web-site design, or no commercial use, private personal use only, etc. Read such injunctions carefully—they are there for a reason.

In the case of fonts, it is generally considered part of the necessity of doing business to provide the fonts used in your documents, to the professional service bureau producing your documents. The service bureau is required to destroy the fonts after they produce your documents; they may not keep them for reuse on someone else's project, unless they purchase licenses from the font foundries that own the copyright on them.

In Conclusion

Finally, we come to the display of the copyright notice. Under current law, such display is not required to protect your work (since, as stated before, you own the copyright—except in the case of work-for-hire projects—when you create it and commit it to tangible form). The typical copyright notice appears once on or within the work (not on every page, as some apprehensive neophytes are compelled to do): copyright symbol, year, author—as in © 2002 Lily Splane. In a book, the copyright notice appears on a special page just for it. Ⓟ may also appear indicating copyright for live performance recordings.

How to Contact the Copyright Office

HTTP://COPYRIGHT.GOV

Library of Congress
Copyright Office
101 Independence Avenue, S.E.
Washington, D.C. 20559-6000
(202) 707-3000 or 1 (877) 476–0778 (toll free)

What Forms to Get

- Form TX—text: literary work, computer programs
- Form VA—visual arts: artwork, photography, architecture
- Form PA—performance arts: choreography, scripts, motion pictures, musical scores
- Form SR—sound recordings
- Form SE—serials, periodicals: magazines, newspaper

Copyright fees are $35.00 per book (electronic submission; $85 for mailed paper form) plus a deposit of two copies of a published work; one copy if unpublished. You may register an *unpublished* collection of work as one piece.

ISBNs

You will be responsible for setting up an account with R.R. Bowker Company, a book tracking company that registers books into international databases for use by libraries, universities, book distributors, and bookstores. You may purchase ISBNs (International Standard Book Numbers) and Barcodes from Bowker. You will place the ISBN barcode on the back cover and verso of the title page (copyright page) for every book you publish. Bookdealers will not accept books for resale without these numbers.

You will also receive a Standard Address Number (SAN) for your publishing company. This number allows easy tracking within the book industry and helps bookstores and distributors find you and your books wherever you publish in the world.

Bowker's fees vary to set up a publisher account with the all the necessary numbers. You may visit R.R. Bowker's website to submit ABI (advance book information) forms, get a SAN assignment, and purchase ISBNs and barcodes:

HTTP://WWW.MYIDENTIFIERS.COM

ISBN Agency
R.R. Bowker Company
121 Chanlon Road
New Providence, NJ 07974-1541

The ISBN is a special code that cannot be imitated or faked, as it is generated through a mathematical calculation and recorded in the world's databases. Big Brother is watching your books.

ISBNs are *always* ten or thirteen digits long. The first three numbers in an ISBN-13 code begin with 978, which indicates the product is a book. The next nine digits in an ISBN actually stand for something (explained later), and the tenth digit is a check digit that is calculated from the other nine digits. The check digit helps detect incorrectly transcribed ISBNs. An *X* is sometimes substituted for 10 as a check digit. The ISBN is multiplied by a *weight digit* from 10 to 2. The total of the products must equal a number evenly divisible by 11. If it is not, then the ISBN is incorrect.

Examine the ISBN 0-945962-08-8

0	9	4	5	9	6	2	0	8	8
10	9	8	7	6	5	4	3	2	
↓	↓	↓	↓	↓	↓	↓	↓	↓	
0	81	32	35	54	30	8	0	16	

Total =264. 264 ÷ 11 = 24. The ISBN is correct.

An ISBN is separated into four groups by hyphens. Three of these groups (the fourth is the check digit) represent information about the publisher and the publisher's titles.

Example: 0-945962-08-8

The first digit (0) is the *group identifier*. It identifies the national or geographical region (United States in our example).

The second group of digits (945962) is the *publisher identifier*. The number of digits in the publisher identifier group indicates the number of books the publisher expects to publish in its lifetime. The more digits, the *fewer books*; fewer digits signifies more books.

Publisher Identifier Table

NUMBERS IN GROUP	BOOKS PUBLISHED
00–19	1,000,000
200–699	100,000
7000–8499	10,000
85000–89999	1,000
900000–949999	100
9500000–9999999	10

If the publisher registers as a ten-book publisher and later grows beyond expectations, an additional ISBN publisher identifier may be assigned.

The third group (08 in our example) identifies the book title. Different bindings (perfect, comb, case-bound) must have a different ISBN with a different title identifier and check digit. Different editions or revisions also must be assigned a new ISBN.

Some books, such as text books and operation manuals, may be accompanied by supplementary texts such as updates and instructor guides. These supplements carry the same ISBN as the "parent" book.

Books with more than one volume have one ISBN for the *whole* set, and a separate ISBN for each *volume* of the set. Supplementary and auxiliary texts carry the same ISBN as the "parent" text. (Examples are software manuals with separate booklets for updates or advanced information.)

CIP Data

If you plan to publish others' books in addition to those you write yourself, you are eligible to have these books registered with the Library of Congress (lab manuals and other "disposable" books and booklets do not qualify). The Library of Congress can assign you Cataloging-in-Publication (CIP) data for inclusion in your books. This service is free of charge. Visit the Library of Congress website or write for forms and instructions for securing preassigned Library-of-Congress catalog numbers. Please note that the Copyright Office and the CIP Office are not the same agency.

HTTP://WWW.LOC.GOV/PUBLISH/CIP/

CIP Office
Library of Congress
Washington, DC 20540

CIP numbers must be procured before a book is published, so this data can be included on the copyright page of the book during typesetting and layout. Some restrictions for Cataloging-in-Publication make certain books ineligible for inclusion:

- Print-on-Demand (POD) books
- Self-Published books (if your book is, however, part of your publishing company which carries other authors' titles, then this rule does not apply)
- Books already published (*except* new editions or major revisions with new ISBNs)
- Books with little text and mostly graphics (art or comic books)
- Books published outside the United States
- Instructional materials, such as textbooks
- Pocket-sized books (most "grocery store" fiction)
- Serials
- E-Books

LCCN Assignments

Books ineligible for CIP data may be assigned a Library of Congress Control Number (LCCN). This will facilitate cataloging and categorization for your book.

This is a great alternative for self-published and print-on-demand books.

BISAC Data

The Book Industry Standards and Communications (BISAC) code is frequently required on the back cover of marketed books. The BISAC code provides a subject and category that facilitates shelving in bookstores and libraries, though many libraries still use the Dewey Decimal System.

The Book Industry Study Group is responsible for over-seeing, expanding, modifying, and maintaining the BISAC database. Visit BISG for more information and complete updated BISAC subject list:

HTTPS://WWW.BISG.ORG

BISAC data is constantly being updated, categories expanded and refined as the topics of written matter demands it. The complete list exceeds 80 pages and includes the foundation list plus several revision lists that modify the base list.

Sample BISAC Data

BISAC Code	Subject/Category/Subcategory .... Sequence
ART030010	ART/Design/Book................................. 83
COM065000	COMPUTERS/Electronic Publishing................. 363
CRA046000	CRAFTS & HOBBIES/Bookbinding.................. 561
FIC027010	FICTION/Romance/Adult 757
LAN005000	LANGUAGE ARTS & DISCIPLINES/ Composition & Creative Writing 1539
PHI005000	PHILOSOPHY/Ethics & Moral Philosophy 2086

Small Press Listings

HTTP://WWW.DUSTBOOKS.COM

Dustbooks
International Directory of
Little Magazines and Small Presses
P.O. Box 100-P
Paradise, CA 95967

You may also want to join a bookseller's organization:

North American Bookdealer's Exchange
P.O. Box 606
Cottage Grove, OR 97427

ISNI—Your *World* Identity

Assigning numbers from different agencies makes your book easier to find in the world of millions of titles. Let's not forget that, in addition to identifying and categorizing your book, *you* need to be identified with your own special International Standard Name Identifier number (ISNI) assignment. This is especially important if you have a common name, such as John Robinson. This database helps differentiate you, the author, from a musician or artist with the same name. Find information and get your ISNI assignment at:

HTTP://WWW.ISNI.ORG

Who's Who

Some authors may also wish to include their names, works, and biographies in *Who's Who* references and databases. These usually charge a fee for inclusion. There are many *Who's Who*-type books in print for specific industries, such as publishers, writers, entertainers, artists, sports figures, scientists, etc. Have fun Googling your way to fame....

Part 2

The Page

t All Happens Here: The Page

Once you've decided approximately how many pages will compose your book, the next step is to decide how the pages will look. Once you decide this, the same formatting will apply across all chapters to create a sense of continuity and wholeness.

In book production lingo, the actual page of a book is called the *ground*. This is the blank area inside the margins where the text appears. The text is called the *figure*.

The very first thing you will want to do is to design a *template* for your book before you import the word processing documents into the page-layout program. Templates make book design easy. While a 5½" by 8½" book of less than 128 pages is best typeset and layed out as one contiguous file, larger books of 8½" by 11" size will probably have to be separated out into several files that can later be linked and printed as a book. A template is a lifesaver in this case: Once you set up a template with margins and styles, it can be used again and again for each file. All pages and all files in your book will have the exact same dimensions and type styles—no having to remember what you did last time. InDesign is very good at this particular task.

InDesign also allows you to set up a single file for 5½" by 8½" books in *sequential half-pages* that can later be made into a book by your pressman. The advantage of sequential half-pages is that you can place your documents on the half-pages one right after another without having to worry about *signature imposition*. It is only after you have completely finished typesetting and proofreading the book that you set up signatures as the press requires (see "Part 10—Book Binding"). Sequential pages are much easier to keep track of than pages that read 2 and 8, 3 and 7, etc., as they read in signatures. A template set in signatures will have you hopping around the file looking for the correct page. Your printing service will impose the pages as needed to create your book.

When you are setting up your document, some layout programs require you to *choose the printer on which you will print your mechanicals* (final printouts from your computer that you will take to the printing press) The printer driver you choose will dictate to your page-layout or word processing program how to set up the document to print on your specific printer. Everything about the file may change—the leading, character spacing, and many other attributes—if you change printer drivers after laying out your book. Pages may reflow and shift, starting and stopping in the wrong places, causing floating LBOs (lines, boxes, and ovals) to misalign. This means you will have to lay out the whole book all over again.

Margins

It may seem to the uninitiated that setting up margins for a book would be a simple task. Not so.

There are many factors you must take into account when setting page margins for your book. You must not only work within your printer margin-tolerances (different on every printer), you must also take into account *binding*, *trim*, and *gripper* tolerances of the press you will send your files to.

Printers vary in margin tolerances. Most laser printers can produce copy as close as ¼" (0.25") from the edge, though some models do not. Check your printer manual. Some inkjet printers have peculiar margins: The sides could be ¼" (.25"), the top ⅓" (.33"), and the bottom ⅔" (0.67"). The orientation of the sheet can change the relative margins. In landscape mode, the right margin in our example then would be ⅔" (0.67")—which is the bottom margin in portrait mode—while the bottom and top are ¼" (.25"), and the left margin becomes ⅓" (.33"). Obviously, when laying out a book, both left and right margins must match—both at least ⅔" (0.67") to balance the pages.

Another tricky thing about some inkjet printers is that they will chop off letters that are a hair past the minimum margins. Italic type leans a bit out of the right margin, so print margins should be increased by 0.02", making the inkjet working right margin for landscape mode 0.69". You must set up the left margin as 0.69" also.

Binding takes a certain amount of the page away from you that you must measure into your margins. Perfect, plastic GBC comb, and wire spiral binding need a ¹/₄" (0.25") binding width.

Perfect-bound books are trimmed ¹/₁₆" (0.0625") on each of three or four sides. These measurements must be calculated into your margins as well.

Large offset presses have a ¹/₄" (0.25") tolerance for grippers (the part of the press that grabs the paper and pulls it through the printing mechanism). Photocopy machine margins are also ¹/₄". Small offset presses have a ³/₈" (0.375") tolerance for grippers.

Ideally, you should have print-run quotations from several presses *before* you start typesetting and laying out your book. Why? You need to know about their presses. The forms at the end of "Part 9—The Printing Press," will serve nicely in getting this information. Choose a press, then lay out your book for the press.

Measurement Conversions

A particularly aggravating thing about most page-layout programs is that the layout screen has rulers that allow you to measure margins accurately, but dialog boxes in document setup ask you to set up margins in decimals. Unless you are some kind of math masochist, you'll need a handy dandy conversion table, like the one below:

Gutters

A *gutter* is the space between two half-pages on a single 8¹/₂" by 11" sheet of paper. The gutter must equal two times the outside margin, plus two times the trim size (if any), plus two times the binding width. That simply means the gutter (or inside margin) is wider than the outside margin. We'll get into more of that, later.

Alleys

Alleys are technically the space between columns of text on a page, set up similar to a newspaper or a magazine (and this book). When two half-pages are printed on a full sheet of paper, the space between the pages is correctly referred to as an alley. But, since we are making books and not newspapers, we will call this space a gutter because most page layout programs do. In InDesign, set your gutter measurements in the *MARGINS AND COLUMNS...* option under the LAYOUT menu.

Handy-Dandy Fraction–to–Decimal Conversion Table

INCHES IN FRACTIONS	INCHES IN DECIMALS
¹/₃₂	0.03125
¹/₁₆	0.0625
³/₃₂	0.09375
¹/₈	0.125
⁵/₃₂	0.015625
³/₁₆	0.1875
⁷/₃₂	0.21875
¹/₄	0.25
⁹/₃₂	0.28125
⁵/₁₆	0.3125
¹¹/₃₂	0.34375
³/₈	0.375
¹³/₃₂	0.40625
⁷/₁₆	0.4375
⁵/₃₂	0.46875
⁹/₁₆	0.5625
¹⁷/₃₂	0.53125
¹/₂	0.50
¹⁹/₃₂	0.59375
⁵/₈	0.625
²¹/₃₂	0.65625
¹¹/₁₆	0.6875
²³/₃₂	0.71875
³/₄	0.75
²⁵/₃₂	0.78125
¹³/₁₆	0.8125
²⁷/₃₂	0.84375
⁷/₈	0.875
²⁹/₃₂	0.90625
¹⁵/₁₆	0.9375
³¹/₃₂	0.9375

Running Headers

The title of your book appearing on every page is called a *running header*. In most page layout programs, you only have to type this in once, place it on the *master pages*, and it will appear magically on every page.

Your running header may be in the same type as the body text of your book, or another font. Running headers are usually the same size or 1–2 points smaller than the body text. If you use 11-point type for body text, you may use 11-, 10-, or 9-point type for the running header (if you use 10-point body-text type, don't go down to 8-point type for the running header—it's too hard to read).

You may bold or italicize the running header—or do both. Small caps also work well in running headers.

The top margin for books seems at first to be deceptively large. It must be wide enough to accommodate running headers, page numbers, and graphics. See the tables later in this section for guidelines.

Running headers look best when centered and placed about ½" down from the top of the page. You may choose to place the title of the book and/or chapter title on the right master page, and the author's name on the left master page for an attractive alternating effect.

If you feel artistic, you can place a small decorative graphic below or at the sides of the running headers.

After placing the running headers and perhaps graphics, you should have *at least ½"* (.50") of blank space between these items and the body of your book.

Folios

The publishing industry refers to page numbers as *folios*. Folios can go on the outside or center of the bottom or top margins. For simplicity, opt for the top outside margin adjacent to the running headers.

All folios in all books follow the same format: odd numbers on the *recto* (right) page, and even numbers on the *verso* (left)—no exceptions!

You can insert folios on the master pages in InDesign by choosing the TYPE menu, INSERT SPECIAL CHARACTER, MARKERS, CURRENT PAGE NUMBER (or press the Alt Shift Ctrl N keys). The folio marker will appear as a letter, depending on how many master pages you have set up. Go to any other page and the correct page number will automatically appear in the upper outside margin. You can change the starting page number any time by choosing DOCUMENT SETUP under the FILE menu. To *refolio* is to renumber the pages.

Make the folios the same size or 1–2 points larger than the body text, and in a different font—the font used for subheadings is common practice.

You may dress up the folios with *em* dashes *thin spaces* (explained later), on each side of the folio, or even add framing graphics such as boxes or circles.

You should folio pages starting at the beginning of the actual body of the book. If you start at the title page, all front matter will be counted as a page—but the page numbers *must not appear on the front-matter pages* (an exception is using Roman numerals for frontmatter). The pages containing the body of the book must be numbered starting *after* the frontmatter: i, ii, iii, iv, v, vi, 7, 8, 9.... In InDesign, you can use multiple master pages, paginating the frontmatter with Roman numerals, and using a separate master page for folios with regular Arabic numerals in the body of your book. If you choose not to folio the frontmatter, InDesign allows you to select the pages from which you want to remove folios (and running headers) by selecting the pages in the Pages panel, then right-clicking and selecting OVERRIDE ALL MASTER PAGE ITEMS (or press the Alt Shift Ctrl L keys when the page is selected). The body of your book may then appear to begin on page 7 or 11, for example. If you want the body of the book to begin on page 1, then the front matter must be put in a separate file *without* page numbers. This is the method reduces complexity with multiple master pages.

Putting it All Together

If all of this sounds far too complicated, and you're about ready to slam this book shut in frustration...

Never fear, help is on the way. Stick with me. When things look their worst is when I'll bail you out with some nifty table or such.

Industry specifications for margins vary somewhat, but two facts remain: Books look best with a larger bottom than top margin, and with *at least* ½" outside margins. You are always free to use wider margins—just realize that wider margins increase page count and therefore, production costs.

The tables below will help you set up your pages for either laser or inkjet printer, comb or perfect binding, and for a small press, rather than a large press (as they are less costly).

Tweak these specifications at your own risk. If you're a beginner, stick to the tables.

Minimum Margins for Perfect- or Comb-Bound 5½" x 8½" Book

	BASE	TRIM	BINDING	TOTAL
Top margin	1.50"	0.0625		1.5625"
Bottom Margin	0.75"	0.0625		0.8125"
Inside Margin	0.50"	0.0625	0.25"	0.8125"
Outside Margin	0.50"	0.0625		0.5625"
Gutter				1.625"

Minimum Margins for Saddle-Stitched 5½" x 8½" Booklet

	BASE	TRIM	BINDING	TOTAL
Top margin	1.50"			1.50"
Bottom Margin	0.75"			0.75"
Inside Margin	0.50"			0.50"
Outside Margin	0.50"			0.50"
Gutter				1.00"

Parts

Arranging a book into four to twenty parts helps the writer organize topics and ideas. It is also a sneaky way to pad-out a slim book.

Parts are usually announced on a *recto* (right-hand, front) page all by themselves, centered vertically and horizontally, with no other text on the page. You may place artwork on the verso, or begin a new chapter (as in this book), or leave it blank so that a new chapter begins on a recto page.

Chapters

All nonfiction books should be divided into chapters. It's easier for you to work on, as chapters help you organize topics and thoughts. Chapters are also psychologically good for readers. Few people like to read, but if the book is sectioned into small, seemingly independent chunks, they will be more likely to buy it. Chapters of six to twenty pages are best. Readers won't feel they have to make a substantial commitment or a huge time investment to read your book—they can take it in small steps, and before they know it, they've finished your book.

Chapters should always begin on a new page, leaving lots of white space (1–3 inches) between the chapter heading and the body text.

Sections

Some books are further separated into sections, as this one is. This format is even more inviting to busy, distracted readers. They can read sections in just a few minutes—between loads of laundry or irate customers.

Sections begin anywhere on the page as long as there are at least two or three lines of body text that will fit below the section heading (subhead). If less than two or three lines fit, the section must begin on the next page. Use your eye to decide.

Special Elements

Handle tables, side-bars, and info boxes with care. Many of these special elements are a big part of page design. Use them consistently and your book will be attractive and accessible to readers. When you use special elements, keep them the *same* throughout your book. Don't typeset tables one way on page 13, and another way on page 144. Keep line weights and shading effects consistent.

Tables

Center tables on the page or column and allow adequate white space above and below them. The margins inside the tables should be as even as possible on all four sides.

Use the appropriate tabs in your tables. The first column of your table will typically be aligned flush left. The other columns may be flush left or centered if they are text; columns of numbers should be aligned with *decimal* tabs.

The text in the tables may be the same size as the body text, or 1–2 points smaller. The font may be the same as body text, or that of the headings, unbolded. Table headers look best set in bold small caps.

Boxes and Side-bars

Place text that you want to stand out or separate from the body of your book, in a *box* or *side-bar* (a long skinny vertical or horizontal box). You may use a plain box, add an interesting border, put a drop shadow behind the box, or shade the entire inside of the box. Use your imagination and your eyes; the design should complement the body of the book, not compete with it. Whatever effects you choose to use, do the same thing throughout your book. See examples below.

This is a nice side-bar with a chiseled drop shadow. It is unobtrusive, yet gets proper reader attention.

Reversed text in a side-bar is very eye-catching and accentuates the reading experience

This outlined box announces itself rather assertively.

"This is a pull-quote type of side-bar with a drop-shadow on the type and box. It gets proper reader attention, and is easy to read."

Initial Caps

You can create interest and drama with large initial caps or drop caps. Use these sparingly: Enlarging the first letter of the first paragraph in a chapter is attractive; any more is obtrusive and amateurish.

The mass of men lead lives of quiet desperation.
　　　—Henry David Thoreau

The mass of men lead lives of quiet desperation.
　　　—Henry David Thoreau

The mass of men lead lives of quiet desperation.
　　　—Henry David Thoreau

Drama

Side rules running down the inside of your page (as in this book), bottom rules along the bottom margin, and small decorative elements add interest and enhance the reading experience. Don't go crazy and overdo it. These can be set up on the master pages in your page-layout template so that they will print on every page of your book.

Part 3

Parts of a Book

Book Parts

Books are set up in an industry-standard format that is best not toyed with. Bookdealers and prospective buyers expect to see certain things in a certain order. If they have to look for the preface, the notice of copyright, or the appendices, they won't be as likely to buy your book. Book buyers for libraries are especially finicky because your book has to be classified by the Dewey Decimal System. The copyright page, the table of contents, and the index help them do this.

The Front Cover

The cover should shout *buy me! I'm exciting, just what you've always wanted! Wouldn't I look good sitting on your bed stand? How can you resist?*

In other words, the book cover literally sells the book, compelling browsers to pick it up and feel it. The cover should have at least two colors (including black) plus white. The title should be big, designed interestingly, and be easy to read. Photographs and color graphics are pretty, but are rarely necessary. Get creative with type: Place shadows behind it, zoom it, warp it, fill it with a photo or texture, run it vertically or in an arc—create interest and your book will be looked at and considered.

Some of these type effects are possible directly in Adobe InDesign, as well as Adobe PhotoShop, Macromedia Freehand, CorelDraw, and Adobe Illustrator, among other graphics programs.

Light-colored nonfiction books sell better than dark-colored books. The reverse is true for war novels, horror, and science fiction.

Lastly, have an interesting title for your book. Boring titles get bypassed on bookstore shelves. Your title needs to be daring, unusual, intriguing, humorous, shocking, promising, sexy—it needs to evoke emotion and grab interest. Go for the action words. *Boat Accident* is less effective than *Capsized*. *Out of Gas* has less impact than *Running on Empty*. Verbs make the action happen right before your eyes.

Potentially dreary subjects can be livened up with the right title. *Bookmaking Manual* is boring; *The Book Book* is not. *Training Cats* is lifeless; *Having Fun with Your Pussy* is not. *An Irishman Emigrates to America* is dull; *Far and Away* is not.

A well-known computer manual is titled *Stop Stealing Sheep*. The title makes it jump out from a shelf crammed with computer books with somber non-nonsense titles. What on Earth could the author mean?

One-word titles are especially irresistible (but somewhat difficult in titling nonfiction). What does Stephen King mean by *Thinner*? What could the book be about?

Front Matter

Front matter is defined as all the extraneous pages that come before the "meat" of the book. These pages are usually not numbered. Front matter consists of the title page, the copyright page, the dedication, the epigraph, the table of contents, the preface, acknowledgments, and the introduction—all in that order. The title page, copyright page, and table of contents are *mandatory* in a book; the preface, introduction, dedication, epigraph, and acknowledgments are optional.

Title Page

The title page contains the title of the book in large attractive type, the subtitle, and the author's name. The publishing company and the city in which the book was published are listed at the very bottom of the title page. Sometimes, the title page looks exactly like the cover, only printed in all black ink. Most often, the title page differs considerably from the flashy design of the cover.

The title page is a recto page and is not numbered.

Copyright Page

The copyright page lists the title of the book again, the year the book was copyrighted—including the copyright © symbol—and who owns the copyright (usually the author). Below the copyright notice appears the ISBN. Below that appears the Library of Congress Cataloging-in-Publication notice or the LC Catalog Number issued by the Library of Congress.

Also included on the copyright page is a disclaimer. The disclaimer protects you from any misunderstanding or misuse of the information in your book. For example, a nutrition book may have a disclaimer stating that "the information is for nutritional purposes only and is not intended as medical advice or as a substitute for medical care." An electronics repair manual may state that "the techniques have been tested and proven safe *if and only if* the instructions are followed as written and not modified." Fiction books frequently include a disclaimer that "the resemblance of any characters to any person living or dead is purely coincidental." People misunderstand and abuse information all the time. Disclaimers can keep you from being blatantly misunderstood, and therefore abused. *Use them.*

Other information on the copyright page may include which printing *(printing* means print-run) the book is in—1ST, 2ND, 99TH. A notice that the book was printed in the United States of America is necessary to qualify for inclusion in many book databases—foreign-printed books are sometimes ineligible. Your printing press may request that its name and address appear on the copyright page. Be gracious and give it to them. A *colophon*—a description of the font and type size used and how it was typeset (linotronic, electronic, etc.)—may also appear. The publisher's logo, name, and address appear at the bottom of the copyright page.

In general, the copyright page is set in a smaller point size than the body of the book, in either the body text font or a sans serif font used elsewhere in the book.

The copyright page is one page only, is verso the title page, and is not numbered.

Dedication

A dedication is a personal note to someone who is special to the author. To dedicate a book to someone means to make them a gift of your effort because they have somehow inspired or influenced you. Dedications take one or a few lines and appear centered vertically and horizontally on a recto page. The dedication page is sometimes blank on the verso and is also unnumbered.

> For Adrian...
> For all the sleepless nights.

Epigraph

An especially appropriate quote or short poem that somehow evokes the essence of the book is called an *epigraph*. Keep in mind that epigraphs are safer to use if they are in the public domain—not copyrighted. Epigraphs appear centered horizontally and vertically on a recto page. The name of author of the poem or quote appears on a separate line, and is flush with the last letter of the longest line in the poem or quote. The verso is sometimes blank, and the page is unnumbered.

> To be able to distinguish between
> a badly- and well-written book is not enough;
> a professor of literature can do that occasionally.
> —*George Moore, 1852–1933*

Table of Contents

The table of contents is one of the most important parts of your book. The table of contents sells the book. Bookdealers and book browsers always go to the table of contents to see what a book's all about and how detailed the book is.

A table of contents should list major sections, chapters, and minor sections within chapters. These should be indented on separate levels with dotted leaders going to the corresponding page numbers aligned flush-right:

The contents will be much easier to read formatted in this manner. Tables, illustrations, and appendices may be listed at the end of the table of contents in separate sections.

The table of contents can take up several pages, usually beginning on a recto page. The table of contents may end on a recto or verso page. If it ends on a recto page, the verso of that page is left blank. Contents pages may be numbered with lowercase Roman numerals, or remain unnumbered.

InDesign has an excellent table–of–contents-generating routine, found at the bottom of the Layout menu. InDesign uses the styles you've already applied to automatically construct the table of contents—remembering the page numbers—and gives you a loaded pointer to drop the contents onto blank pages.

If your book is separated into many files, you will need to create a NEW BOOK document from the FILE MENU. This new book file allows you to set up a *book list* that InDesign uses to generate the table of contents and to compile your files into one seamless file to print or convert to PDF. Make sure your book list has the files in the order they will appear in the book, i.e., chapter 1, chapter 2, chapter 3, etc.

Preface

The preface is another powerful book-selling tool. The preface is a concise summary of what the book is about and what the book will *do for the reader*. It should be written in a hard-hitting, this-book-will-change-your-life fashion. The preface is the advertisement, the hook that gets the readers' expectations whipped into a froth. The preface asserts that your particular approach to the subject is unique and far better than in "all those other trashy tomes."

Prefaces are frequently written by someone other than the author—preferably someone famous who just loves your book, or is at least willing to fake it.

The preface begins on a recto page and may be longer than a single page, but it is a better selling tool if it is limited to a single page. The pages are not numbered, and the verso is left blank if the preface ends on a recto page.

Acknowledgments

People who help you with your book—researchers, typists, compositors, graphics artists, therapists—deserve an acknowledgment by the author—a "thank-you-for-making-my-life-easier" notice.

Acknowledgments begin on a recto page and may run from one to several pages, depending how much input you actually needed on the book.

Acknowledgment pages are not numbered, and if they end on a recto page, the verso is left blank.

Introduction

The introduction serves to ease the reader into the subject matter of your book without too much fuss. Introductions may include some basic preliminary explanations of terms used, a short primer on basics required to understand the subject, or a breakdown of how the book is to be used. It is in the introduction that you may mention that the chapters must be read sequentially or the reader can skip around at will, that certain college courses are required to understand the rest of the book, or that particular terms are used in special ways and are to be understood as such.

Introductions may also include a short history of the subject, and the current state of the subject. They may include an explanation of the author's motives for writing the book (besides monetary greed). In short, introductions are the consummate segue from title page to the meat of the matter.

The pages of the introduction may be numbered along with the body of the book, numbered with lowercase Roman numerals, or kept unnumbered. Introductions should begin on a recto page. If the introduction ends on a recto page, the first chapter may begin on the verso, or the verso may be left blank so the chapter begins on the next recto page. It's your call.

Back Matter

Back matter is the stuff that's necessary to make a book complete, but would get in the way if it were put anywhere but in the back.

Appendix

The appendix includes important facts—sometimes technical information—that is necessary for a complete understanding of the subject of your book, but won't be missed by those lacking adventure and initiative (i.e., most people). You can have more than one appendix. Appendices include formulas, tables, glossaries, and other collections of facts that the intellectually starved drool over. You may have as many appendices as you can afford to cram in your book. Appendices start on a new page after the end of the book body—either recto or verso, and are titled with Roman numerals or capital letters. Appendices are usually listed in the table of contents in a separate small list.

Bibliography

The bibliography (recto or verso) is the part of the book where you impress your readers with how much research you've done to write your book. An *annotated bibliography* is a list of references that are coded with superscripts throughout the text—it lets people actually track down where you got your harebrained ideas.

Annotated bibliographies are difficult to compile, and for the most part are unnecessary unless you intend to self-publish scholarly works that will be used by researchers in your field.

A simple list of references will suffice for the average book. It is enough that you can show you've done your homework and know of what you write. A bibliography provides important resources for readers who would like more information on your subject.

Do not alter the conventions of citing references. Set each citation with a ¼" (.25") to ⅓" (.34") hanging indent The author's last name appears first, first name and middle initial last with a period. Set the book title and subtitle in italics. Separate the subtitle from the title with a colon. The city in which the book was published appears next, then a colon, then the name of the publishing company, followed by the year the book was published. If an author is cited twice with different titles, insert two em dashes instead of his/her name a second time.

If the source is a magazine, list the title of the article in lowercase (with an initial cap) between quotes and italicize the magazine name. After the magazine name, list the volume number, the month in parentheses, a colon and the pages. Examples are below:

Cretin, Ima. *The Fall of the Roamin' Empire: Was it a Hoax?* San Diego: Brainrash and Sons, 1994

——. *Who's Afraid of Ghandi?* San Diego: Brainrash and Sons, 1992

Moron, Mandy. "How to impress friends by blowing milk through your nose," *Scientific Diversions* 13(4):121–126

Index

An index is important in nonfiction books. Many word processors and page-layout programs have indexing routines. Believe it or not, computer-generated indexes don't take any less time and aren't any less frustrating than indexing by hand. Do not index your manuscript in a word processor before importing files to a page-layout program. The page imposition will be different in a page-layout program.

Face it: Indexing is a bitch. What's worse is you can't even begin until your whole book is typeset and layed-out, and you have it alive and throbbing in your hands... *a book! It's alive! A book!*

Well, not quite. Now comes the hard part. Indexing is the very last step you will take before sending your book to press. You will be working from a hard-copy printout (page proofs) from your computer.

The first thing to consider is the reader. What words will readers try to look up, and how will they look them up? Pick significant words, circling or highlighting them with a marker on each page. Don't worry about repeaters at this point. After you've done this, go get a big stack of index cards. Now comes the fun part.

Beginning with the first page, copy each highlighted word onto an index card, along with the page number where it appears— writing *one* word on *each* card. Indicate whether the entry is a *main* entry or a primary or secondary *subentry* that goes under the main entry. Continue with all the pages until you've copied each word and corresponding page number onto an index card.

Alphabetize the cards. Now go through the alphabetized stack, note page numbers, and remove all word and page repeaters. Next, find all entries that belong together—mark the entries as main, primary subentry, or secondary subentry. Alphabetize the groups of main and subentries. You now have a coherent stack of cards from which to type a list.

Index formatting also follows certain standards. The main entry is flush left, the primary subentry is indented one em space, the secondary subentry is indented two em spaces. These *ems* may be inserted from the TYPE MENU, *INSERT WHITE SPACE* option. Or if stuck in a word processor, you may use ¼" tabs. Use initial caps for main entries; type subentries in all lowercase:

> Rafts, 206
> inflatable, 207

Always list the entire page number where the entry can be found. If the word or topic appears in a range of pages type the first page number, an en dash, and the last page number where it is found. If the topic is found on non-sequential pages, type the first page number, a comma, a space, and the other page number on which it is found. Page numbers must always be in numerical sequence. When a main entry has no page number, follow it with a colon.

Alphabetize all subentries under the main entry, ignoring prepositions (in, of, at). Do not use prepositions if it would change the meaning of the entry:

> Carpenter's level, 25

does not mean the same as...

> Carpenter
> level of, 25

Cross-reference entries that might be looked for under another topic or are commonly abbreviated. Indicate cross-referencing with the italicized *See* or *See also*. Align a cross-reference with the entry above it:

> Corn, 376
> mush, 377
> *See also* grits

Alphabetize abbreviations such as *Mr., Mt.,* and *St.* as if spelled out in full. Alphabetize *Mac* and *Mc* prefixes as if they are all *Mac*—that's where the reader will look for them. Include articles (the, a) in entries only if they are part of a proper name:

> Washington Post, The, 92

Foreign words and names are tricky. Alphabetize words beginning in *L'* or *O'* must be alphabetized as beginning with *L* or *O*—as if no apostrophe exists.

> O'Kelly, 77
> Okra, 30
> soup, 34
> O'Malley, 78–81, 84
> Omar, 201

Author Bio

The author biography is usually found towards the back of the book in plain sight of the curious. But, it is not so flagrantly conspicuous as to earn accusations of conceit from the hypersensitive. Keep the bio short and pertinent—mention any education or experience that qualifies you to write the book, and maybe a factoid or two regarding your personal life—in what city you reside, if you're married and have kids, or if you dress your cats in Chatty-Kathy doll clothes. Whatever. Keep it simple.

The Spine

If you perfect-bind your book, the width of the book spine will be determined by the *caliper* of the paper and cover you will use for your book. (See the "Paper Caliper" section in "Part 8—Paper".) You must have this information before you design the spine copy.

All text must run *down* the spine, not up it. This is a common mistake with novices. The text will read correctly if the book is laid flat, cover up.

Folding accuracy of covers during binding varies. For this reason, leave some space between the edge of the book and the words. You may set up your spine as part of the front or back page if your book will be 5½" by 8½"; set the spine up on a separate sheet for 8½" by 11" books.

The Back Cover

The back cover is yet another opportunity to sell your book. On it, you may want a short titillating summary of what your book is about, or you may be influential enough to garner praise from famous people. If you can get well-known people to read your book, by all means do it and then ask for comments to use as back-cover or jacket blurbs. Comments from other authors, celebrities, college professors, doctors, even local professionals can do wonders for sales. Keep in mind to get comments from people who are experts in the same field as your book. A jacket blurb from Martha Stewart for your carpentry book is inappropriate. Martha Stewart is not a recognized expert on carpentry—Bob Villa is, and that's who you'll want blurbs from.

Pre-publication praise from those of influence will, of course, have to be procured before you publish the book. That means you send people the *galley proofs*, preferably bound for easier handling. After the book is finished, send a free copy to everyone who was good enough to read your galley proofs—whether or not they provided comments you found useful.

Also, never underestimate the value and power of layperson testimonials. Everyday Joe Blows like to air their opinions, and especially like seeing their comments and names in print. Do you know people who could use your book? Give them a bound copy of the galley proofs and ask them for their opinions and suggestions. You'll have more testimonials than you can possibly use. Be sure to send them a nice shiny new copy of your book when it's off the press.

Barcodes

Barcoding is becoming an industry standard. Failure to use barcodes can leave many small-time self-publishers with an overstock if they aren't prepared to put out the little extra effort to comply. Bookstores and distributors alike are increasingly dependent on point-of-sale inventory and cash-flow records. Bar codes allow them to keep accurate records of stock and how much money they owe publishers.

Bookland EAN barcodes are not the same as the standard code 39 you see on most merchandise in department or grocery stores. EAN codes have the ISBN encrypted in the code, and an additional code indicates the cover price. Barcodes makes inventory and payment easy and nearly foolproof. (I say *nearly* because anything that can be built by a human can be undone by a fool.)

In the Bookland EAN, barcodes must be accompanied by human-readable characters, in not less than 10-point type. The OCR A font was designed specifically to be both human- and machine-readable.

In an EAN, the ISBN is preceded by 978. Following 978 is the group identifier, publisher identifier, and the title identifier. The check digit (last digit in the ISBN) is recalculated using matrix mathematics that is somewhat involved.

Calculating the EAN from the ISBN

Enter the ISBN:	0-945962-08-8
Drop the check digit:	0-945962-08
Drop hyphens, add the EAN flag:	**9 7 8 0 9 4 5 9 6 2 0 8**
Add weighting factors:	1 3 1 3 1 3 1 3 1 3 1 3

Multiply EAN by factors:	9 21 8 0 9 12 5 27 6 6 0 24
Sum the products:	= 127
Divide by 10:	= 12.7
Subtract the whole number, leaving the decimal:	-12, = remainder 7

The remainder is the digit you use to look up the *new* check digit from the table below.

EAN Check Digit

REMAINDER	EAN CHECK DIGIT	REMAINDER	EAN CHECK DIGIT
0	0	5	5
1	9	6	4
2	8	7	3
3	7	8	2
4	6	9	1

The new check digit for our example (978094596208) is 3.

The complete EAN will read 9780945962083 and will be encrypted into the barcode.

Next to the book barcode is the price code. If a cover price is set, the first two digits are always 50 for a book under $10.00; the first digit is 5 for books $10.00 and over. This means that a $9.95 book would be coded 50995, and a $24.95 book would be coded 52495. Simple.

If the price is not set and may be determined by the bookseller, a code 90000 is used instead to indicate a variable price.

Sounds pretty hairy doesn't it? Aren't you glad you have a computer?

Bookland EAN bar codes can be purchased from barcoding companies such as R.R. Bowker, or printed directly from your computer with appropriate software. CorelDraw includes a great barcode generator. Special fonts in the OCR family, and plugins for your layout program may also be used to generate barcodes for your books.

Human-Readable ISBN 10

ISBN 0-945962-14-2

9 780945 962144   5 2 4 9 5 ——— Price

Sample ISBN Barcode

ISBN

At-A-Glance Page-Content Table

RECTO	VERSO
FRONTMATTER	
Title Page	
	Copyright Page
Dedication Page	
Epigraph	
Table of Contents	
Preface	
Acknowledgements	
Introduction	
Major Section	
Chapter Beginning	Chapter Beginning
BACKMATTER	
Appendix	Appendix
Bibliography	Bibliography
Author Bio	Author Bio

Part 4

Fantastic Fonts

Fonts

This chapter encompasses almost everything you think you don't need to know about fonts. The truth is, without an understanding of font families and font styles, you could end up with an amateurish nightmare that won't sell.

Font Types

Fonts have three sources: the printer's internal fonts (text mode or *hard* fonts), a font cartridge, and software (downloadable or *soft* fonts). Soft fonts are printed using the printer's graphic mode.

Fonts show themselves in two forms: hardcopy printout and screen. Printed fonts are described with dots; screen fonts are described with light pixels. Though most computers claim WYSIWYG (what-you-see-is-what-you-get), it is an illusion that you print out what's on the screen. Your printer resolution is usually much higher than screen resolution—at least if you're not limping along on a 9-pin dot matrix printer. Your screen resolution is approximately 72–96 dpi (some HD monitors as high as 120 dpi), whereas your printer may be as high as 1200 dpi (or higher on some inkjet printers), and PostScript fonts (the typesetting industry standard) are encoded with information to print out at up to 2540 dpi on a Linotronic imagesetter.

Fonts are stored on your hard drive in two parts. The *font data* are simple bits and bytes that describe the font. The *font header* is the information about the font at the beginning of a font file; this is where the font name, spacing, and kerning data are stored.

Fonts may be either of the *bitmap* or *vector* kind. Vector fonts are stored as mathematical equations describing the edges of the font. These fonts are *scalable* (can be resized without losing resolution) and very smooth.

Computer printers have varying abilities to smooth fonts. They do this in several ways:

- *Aliasing* improves the quality of the printed font by arranging the number of dots in a curve or diagonal stroke. The more dots, the smoother the edges.
- *Color-aliasing* uses grayscale technology to blur and smooth the edges of the font with shades of gray. Ink jet printers do this well.
- *Hinting* is a scaling intelligence that alters fonts at printout to improve the quality. This is especially noticeable with small fonts—the font is altered to keep letters such as *e* and *a* from closing up.

Other smoothing technologies that enhance edge definition may be specific to the brand of printer.

Parts of a Vector-Based Character

Each character in a vector-based font has certain attributes. The *stroke* of a character is the outline that defines the character. The *baseline* is where the base of an uppercase character sits. The *ascender* is the portion of the character that extends above the baseline. The *ascender space* extends above the *x-height* to make room for diacritical marks. The *descender* is the portion of a lowercase character that extends below the baseline.

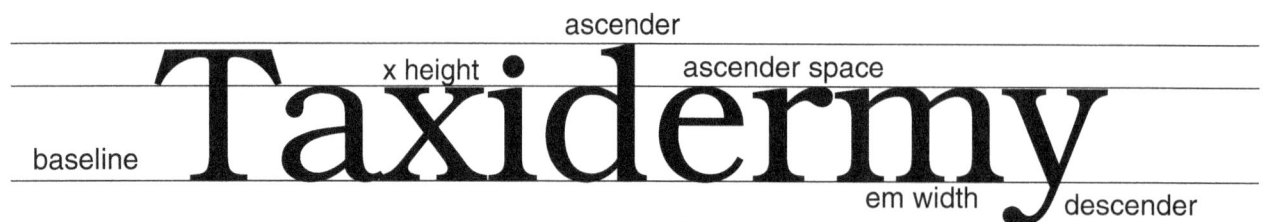

ascender

x height • ascender space

Taxidermy

baseline

em width descender

Other Kinds of Fonts

Bitmap fonts are rendered as dots or pixels. Though they can be magnified and smoothed, they are not scalable—resizing them greatly reduces resolution quality.

You may sometimes hear about *text fonts*. Text fonts are bitmap internal fonts found in some printers—especially the dot-matrix kind. They are not scalable and usually come in 10-point size in pica (10 characters per inch—cpi), and elite (12 cpi). They resemble typewriter output. The character width and spacing may further be manipulated by *condensing* and *expanding* pica or elite type. Condensed pica type is 15 cpi; expanded is 5 cpi. Condensed elite type is 17 cpi; expanded is 6 cpi.

Measurement Systems

Fonts are sized in *points*—either hardwired as in a bitmap font, or scalable to any size as in a vector-based font. One point is $1/72$" or 0.1388888". Unfortunately for us, point size can be determined by two methods: by measuring the distance of the full caps size *plus* descenders and ascenders, or by full caps only. The most common method is the former.

To further confuse the issue, some measurement systems use the *pica*, which is equal to $1/6$ of an inch (six picas make an inch). One point is $1/12$ of a pica (6 picas make 72 points, which is an inch). Pica measurement is often used in page-layout programs for not only fonts, but even ruler-guide measurements. We won't be using picas; they scare people.

Examples of Common Point Sizes

6 point

7 point

8 point

9 point

10 point

11 point

12 point

13 point

14 point

15 point

16 point

18 point

24 point

30 point

36 point

48 point

60 point

72 point

Points–to–Inches Conversion Table

Point	Inch	Point	Inch
2	0.03	52	0.72
4	0.06	**54**	**0.75**
6	0.08	56	0.78
8	0.11	58	0.81
10	0.14	60	0.83
12	0.17	62	0.86
14	0.19	64	0.89
16	0.22	66	0.92
18	**0.25**	68	0.95
20	0.28	70	0.97
22	0.31	**72**	**1.00**
24	0.33	74	1.03
26	0.36	76	1.06
28	0.39	78	1.08
30	0.42	80	1.11
32	0.44	82	1.14
34	0.47	84	1.17
36	**0.50**	86	1.20
38	0.53	88	1.22
40	0.56	**90**	**1.25**
42	0.58	92	1.28
44	0.61	94	1.31
46	0.64	96	1.33
48	0.67	98	1.36
50	0.70	100	1.39

Human-World Point–to–Inch Conversions

9 points =	⅛"
18 points =	¼"
24 points =	⅓"
28 points =	⅜"
36 points =	½"
46 points =	⅝"
48 points =	⅔"
54 points =	¾"
64 points =	⅞"
72 points =	1"
80 points =	1¼"
94 points =	1⅓"

Font Families

A font is an entire type *family* having the same letter shape. Fonts impart emotional content. They can be elegant, romantic, humorous, or friendly, while others look cold, technical, or businesslike. Some fonts are a blend of emotions.

Courier—resembling typewriter output—is commonly used in the legal profession because it is familiar, straightforward, and is devoid of emotional content (unlike the courtrooms where Courier is used).

Old English, *Park Avenue*, and *Boulevard* are elegant fonts. They impart feelings of serious respect, even arrogance. These fonts are used on university degrees, certificates, and rich people's business cards.

The romantic fonts include *Coronet*, **Brush Script** and *Zapf Chancery*. They are elegant, beautiful fonts resembling calligraphy. They are suited well to formal invitations, personal announcements, and thank-you notes.

Comic Sans, Ransom, and Benguiat Frisky are playful fonts. They convey humor and a lighthearted feeling.

Poppl-Laudatio, **Hobo**, **Impress**, and DomCasual are friendly, relaxed, informal fonts.

Cold, technical fonts include Tech, LCD, and OCR-A fonts. They appear as if produced by a digital machine for other machines to read.

Gill Sans and Universe Condensed are often seen in business correspondence and spreadsheets.

All of the aforementioned fonts are unsuitable for typesetting books. Book fonts such as **Times**, **Palatino**, Garamond, **Baskerville**, **New Century Schoolbook**, and **Bookman** are no-nonsense fonts. They are time-honored and traditional body-text fonts developed for their readability.

Goudy Old Style is a common book font that blends a no-nonsense attitude with a nostalgic, old-fashioned flavor. Goudy Old Style looks as if it were printed in the late 1800s.

Helvetica and Avant Garde are serious but not-too-stuffy fonts that are best used as headings, rather than as body text in a book.

Your choice of fonts is critical to conveying the message. You wouldn't want to typeset a consumer-complaint letter in Old English, set a book in OCR, invite guests to your wedding in Courier, or announce a funeral with Ransom. In short, your message is not just in the words, but in how the words *look*.

> **𝕯ear 𝕾irs:**
> 𝕴 take exception with your policy regarding the finality of sales. "𝕴f it breaks, you own both parts" is not commensurate with acceptable business practices in this county.
>
> You are cordially invited to witness the marriage of our daughter, Ms. Ella Vader to her beloved Mr. Oliver Clozeoff on February 29ᵀᴴ, 2002 at 2:00 P.M.
>
> In Memoriam of Jason Katz Service to be Held in the Bereavement Wing of the Our Lady of Eternal Anguish Church

Serif and Sans Serif Fonts

Serif fonts have little hooks and feet on them. Serif type leads the eye to the next letter and is easier to read than *sans serif* type—type without serifs. Serif fonts are used in the body text of most books.

Always choose type for readability and/or space conservation. Browse the lists on this page.

Popular Serif Fonts

Bookman	Palatino
Bookman italic	*Palatino italic*
Bookman bold	**Palatino bold**
Bookman bold italic	*Palatino bold italic*

Bernhard Modern	New Century Schoolbook
Bernhard Italic	*N. C. Schoolbook italic*
Bernhard Bold	**N. C. Schoolbook bold**
Bernhard Bold Italic	***N.C. Schoolbook bold italic***

Baskerville	Times
Baskerville italic	*Times italic*
Baskerville bold	**Times bold**
Baskerville bold italic	***Times bold italic***

Garamond	Goudy Old Style
Garamond italic	*Goudy Old Style Italic*
Garamond bold	**Goudy Old Style Bold**
Garamond bold italic	**Goudy OS Bold Italic**

Popular Sans Serif Fonts

Sans serif type is often used as *display* type. Display type is chapter headings, subheadings, artwork captions, and *callouts* (labels in a diagram or other graphic).

AvantGarde	Gill Sans
AvantGarde oblique	*Gill Sans oblique*
AvantGarde bold	**Gill Sans bold**
AvantGarde bold oblique	***GillSans bold oblique***

Helvetica	Univers
Helvetica italic	*Univers oblique*
Helvetica bold	**Univers bold**
Helvetica bold italic	***Univers bold oblique***
Helvetica Narrow	Univers Condensed

Eurostile	Futura
Eurostile oblique	*Futura italic*
Eurostile bold	**Futura bold**
Eurostile bold oblique	***Futura bold italic***

Italics are actually a change in letter shape as well as posture. Sans serif fonts are set in *oblique*, rather than italics. Because of the angular strokes, bolding some sans serif fonts can close up the space between letters.

Decorative Fonts

As with all fonts, decorative type imparts *attitude,* expressing the unconscious emotional intention of the writing. Decorative fonts are rarely used in book making, but lend themselves well to book covers. Otherwise, they are best reserved for flyers, brochures, newsletters, and wedding invitations.

ANNA   IGLOO
ALGERIAN   Jurassic
Asimov   BLOODY
Mistral   Broadway
OregonWet   Comic Sans
PepperMint   CAVEMAN
Poseidon   CHILI PEPPER
Ransom Paste   Certificate
Satanick   Kuniefont
Staccato   SCRIBA
STEELWOLF   Giddyup
STONE AGE   GREECE
Dancin   HEADHUNTER
Arriba Arriba   UMBRA

Script Fonts

Author   Brush Script
Commercial Script   Coronet
Black Chancery   Arabian
Lydian Cursive   Marriage Script
Matura   Staccato555
Park Avenue   Pepita
Script   Signet Roundhand
Vivaldi   Zapf Chancery

Avoid italicizing decorative or script fonts—it makes them grotesque. Also avoid using all caps in decorative fonts—they are much too hard to read:

Brush Script   Old English
BRUSH SCRIPT   OLD ENGLISH

How Thrifty is Your Font?

Some fonts take up more space than others. An important factor in choosing fonts is not only readability, but space constraints. Will the book need to be padded-out, or slimmed down? The more pages your book has, the higher the production costs. The slimmer your book, the lower the perceived value and the lower the cover price will have to be to sell it. Find a font that will allow a nice balance between these two concerns.

Garamond (PostScript version) is the most space-conservative font, hence its popularity. Using Garamond as a standard, compare the space requirements of other popular serif fonts, set in 11-point type:

GARAMOND:
Compare sentence length.

TIMES:
Compare sentence length.

GOUDY OLD STYLE:
Compare sentence length.

PALATINO:
Compare sentence length.

NEW CENTURY SCHOOLBOOK:
Compare sentence length.

BOOKMAN:
Compare sentence length.

FONT	% MORE SPACE USED THAN WITH GARAMOND			
	10 PT	11 PT	12 PT	AVERAGES
Times	2.5%	2%	9%	4.5%
Goudy Old Style	2.5%	4.5%	10%	5.5%
Palatino	7.5%	11%	12%	10%
N. C. Schoolbook	15%	13%	12%	12%
Bookman	15%	15%	21%	17%

From these tables we can easily see that Times is the next space-conservative font (compared to Garamond), followed by Goudy Old Style, Palatino, and New Century Schoolbook.

Bookman is a space hog. If you need to pad-out your book, this is the font to use. Twelve-point Bookman will eat up pages if the word count is so low that your book would look like a brochure if set in 10-point Garamond. You'd have to sell such a "brochure" at a cover price higher than its perceived value to buyers. Use fonts wisely—it'll pay off in the end.

Type Styles

Fonts can further be subclassified by *weight, posture,* and *tracking*. These subclasses are commonly referred to collectively as *type styles*.

The weight of a font is the thickness of the stroke as compared to normal or regular weight. The posture of the font describes whether it leans or not, and how much. Small caps is sometimes considered a posture because it is a squatty version of normal type. Tracking refers to the spacing between the letters. In InDesign and other page layout programs, it is adjustable by percent, whereas in most word processors, you get three choices: normal, expanded, and condensed. Tracking is detailed in "Part 5—Banzai Typesetting."

Weight	Posture	Tracking
regular	*italic*	normal
medium	roman	condensed
bold	oblique	expanded
light	Small Caps	narrow

These type styles all have their specific uses in bookmaking. As with font families, type styles should not be used indiscriminately, but with care as described in "Part 5—Banzai Typesetting."

Fonts That Work Well Together

In choosing fonts for books, you will need two fonts: one for the body text, and another for headings. For a polished, professional look, choose a serif font for body text and a sans serif font for headings.

You will use different sizes of the san serif font, depending on the *level* of the heading. Sub-headings are typically smaller than the main heading. More on headings in the "Part 5—Banzai Typesetting" chapter.

The publishing-industry standby pair is Times with Helvetica. This is fine for e-books, but consider a more eclectic pair to make your book stand out. The following table by no means indicates you must adhere to these pairs: choose your own combination if you have strong preferences. In general, choose a sans serif font for headings that has a heavier stroke than the body-text serif font, especially when bolded. Look for a complimentary font that does not dominate and overpower the body-text font, and likewise, does not look wimpy and cowering against an assertive body-text font.

Body Text	Headings
Times	Helvetica
Aldine	Arial Rounded
New Century Schoolbook	Avant Garde
Garamond	Kabel
Baskerville	Futura
Palatino	Gothic
Nicolas Cochin	Lydian
Bernhard Modern	Antiquarian
Book Antiqua	Impact
Bookman OldStyle	Parade
Bruce OldStyle	Prima Sans
Cambria	Goudita Sans Heavy
Caslon	Segoe
Goudy OldStyle	Clarity Gothic
High Tower Text	Abadi
Body Text	Headings

Body Text	Headings
Industrial736	**Kartika**
Minion Pro	**Myriad Pro**
Modern No.20	**Napa**
Sylfaen	**Xpress Heavy**
Vani	**Tahoma**
Zapf Elliptical	**Zapf Humanist**
Zolano Serif	**Boulder**

Bad Font Pairings

Below, find a few examples of some questionable font pairings. The visual impact of these poor marriages is all too apparent.

Body Text	Headings
Garamond	**Goudita Sans Heavy**

Garamond's stroke is quiet fine. The heading font is too heavy for the body-text font.

Nicolas Cochin	**Parade**

Nicolas Cochin is a fine and elegant font. The heading font is too heavy for the body-text font.

Bernhard Modern	**Prima Sans**

Bernhard Modern's stroke is quiet fine. The heading font is too heavy for the body-text font.

Bookman OldStyle	Lydian

Bookman OldStyle needs a more assertive heading font. Lydian is too dainty to pair with it.

High Tower Text	**Boulder**

High Tower Text has a fine stroke with a naturally relaxed tracking. The heading font is too heavy for the body-text font.

Font Names

Within the publishing industry, identical or near-copies of fonts may be found by many names. Most of the names used in this book refer to classic Adobe PostScript versions, or OpenType versions found pre-installed on modern computers. Many font foundries produce copies of standard PostScript fonts to evade licensing issues. Some of the fonts listed below have TrueType "dopplegangers" or even substitutes that will serve you well. It's just a matter of finding them—sometimes for free—online or in font sets included in commercial software, such as CorelDraw® or WordPerfect®.

Times (PostScript font)	Times New Roman (OpenType font)
Helvetica, Helvetica Narrow (PostScript font)	Arial, Arial Narrow (OpenType font)
GREECEBLACK (TrueType font)	LITHOGRAPH (TrueType font)
Arabian (PostScript font)	Flourish, Gelfing (TrueType fonts)
Black Oak (OpenType font)	Wide Latin (OpenType font)
GOLDMINE (PostScript font)	VINETA (OpenType font)
University Roman (PostScript font)	Opera (TrueType font)
TypoUpright (TrueType font)	French Script (OpenType font)
AMATIVE (TrueType font)	Bees Knees (TrueType font)
Amelia (OpenType font)	Asimov (TrueType font)
Barbe Display (PostScript font)	BROADWAY (TrueType font)

Part 5

Banzai Typesetting

The Professional Look

Body Text

A serif type is best for the body of the book—as described in Part 3, serif type is easiest to read.

Type should be 10–12 points (11-point type is popular), and mixed lower and uppercase. Smaller type is difficult to read; larger type makes your book look like a second-grade reader, and may leave your buyers thinking they are being cheated because there are visibly fewer words per page.

10-POINT TYPE:
small—can be taxing on eyesight, especially for older readers
11-POINT TYPE:
medium—comfortable for most readers
12-POINT TYPE:
large—highly readable
14-POINT TYPE:
big—for the visually impaired
18-POINT TYPE:
huge—first-grade reader

Books of 5½" by 8½" size are most readable when line length is kept at 7–9 words per line. Humans can see three or four words per eye movement, and two eye movements per line are less fatiguing. There is an average of six characters in a word, so there will be 45–55 characters per line in a typical book. Large-sized books usually look best and are most readable when typeset in columns, as this book is.

To Justify or Not...

The pages of a book are almost always justified. Justified books, in which both left and right margins are flush and even, look professional and aesthetically appealing. Justifying body text will also save space in higher-end page-layout programs.

If you are stubborn and insist on left-aligning text, leaving a ragged right margin, keep the lines as even as possible. This may involve putting soft returns ([Shift][Enter] in Windows, or [Shift][↵] on the Mac) in strategic places within lines to force them to wrap evenly.

You may typeset side-bars and special elements ragged-right. Ragged right is also acceptable with text-wrap around an object. Ragged-right works best with these items because the smaller the space, the more likely unsightly gaps will occur between words when long words are wrapped to the next line.

Industry-standard is to justify columns. Columns may look best, however, if ragged-right. The words in a narrow justified column rarely space or wrap attractively. See the "Newspaper Columns" section later.

A Matter of Case

Always set your books in both upper and lower case. *Never* use all capitals in words for emphasis—that's what italics are for. Words in all caps in body text are the hallmark of an amateur.

Capitalization is also discouraged in most headings and subheadings. All caps are hard to read; if your titles are long, it is best to set them mixed upper- and lowercase. All caps have to be read one character at a time, rather than as a whole word with a recognizable shape.

An exception is the part or chapter heading. Whether you use all caps for these items will depend on the *length* of the part or chapter title. If the heading is only one line with a few words, all caps may not be all that offensive.

CHAPTER 2: FALLING AND LANDING

Chapter 2: Falling and Landing

CHAPTER 15

Chapter 15

Paragraphs

Paragraphs should be defined with hard returns only and may be either flush-left or indented. If the paragraphs are indented, leave *no space* between paragraphs. If the paragraphs are flush left, add space between paragraphs. Useful spacing is between 0.05" and 0.1". This space can be adjusted for purposes of copyfitting, but should not vary greatly from page to page (keep within 0.03"). Spacing between paragraphs should *never* vary on the same page.

Never mix both techniques. Choose one format and stick with it throughout your book.

> This paragraph is indented; so is the next paragraph.
> Next paragraph—no white-space between.
>
> Do not indent *and* add white-space between paragraphs!
>
> This is a typesetting faux pas that marks your book as non-professional.

Indents

Paragraph indents have traditionally been the width of an em space, but are ¼" (.25") to ⅓" (.34") most commonly. Use the *indent command* in your word processor or page-layout program; *do not use tabs*—tabs will not allow paragraphs to automatically indent with every return. By no means use the spacebar to indent—it won't work with proportional type!

> This paragraph is indented with one em space. Notice how the lines wrap to the next line.
>
> This paragraph is indented with a ¼" indent (as in this book). These indents make text easier to follow.
>
> This paragraph is indented with ⅓" indent. It is also easy to read, but will take up slightly more space.

Never use indents with paragraphs separated by white space, only with text set *without* space between paragraphs. The first paragraph of a chapter is sometimes aligned flush left (unindented) in modern books.

Another kind of indent is a *hanging indent*. This indent is actually a *negative* indent allowing multiple lines of text to wrap below the text rather than the bullet, number, or other object starting the paragraph (see "Bullets and Numbering" section later in this chapter).

> • This paragraph is set off with a bullet. It is created with a hanging indent.

Hanging indents are also used in most bibliographies:

> Flail, Nancy. *How I Overcame My Fear of Knives and Married a Butcher,* San Diego: Brainrash and Sons, 1992.

You will also need to use hanging indents for headlines and boxed text that has punctuation. Quotation marks and ending punctuation should *hang away* from the block of text so that the type aligns properly.

> "This paragraph is set in a small block. Notice how the text aligns and how the quotation marks appear."
>
> "This paragraph looks better balanced. The opening quotation mark is set off with a hanging indent so that the text following it forms a well-aligned block."

Leading

Leading (named from the old-time practice of drawing strips of hot *lead* between rows of metal type) is the space between lines. Industry standard leading is 120% of the point size of the type you are using. This means that 10-point type will have 12 points of leading, and is written as 10/12 in typesetter's shorthand. Eleven point type will have 13.2 leading, written as 11/13; twelve point type will have 14.4 leading, written as 12/14. In page-layout programs, auto leading is the default—that is, it is set at 120% (unless you manually change it) of whatever the size font you use.

At-a-Glance Autoleading Table

TYPE POINTS	AUTO- LEADING	TYPE POINTS	AUTO- LEADING
6	7.2	44	52.8
7	8.4	46	55.2
8	9.6	48	57.6
10	12	50	60
11	13.2	52	62.4
12	14.4	54	64.8
13	15.6	56	67.2
14	16.8	58	69.6
15	18	60	72
16	19.2	62	74.4
18	21.6	64	76.8
20	24	66	79.2
22	26.4	68	81.6
24	28.8	70	84
26	31.2	72	86.4
28	33.6	80	96
30	36	90	108
32	38.4	100	120
34	40.8	120	144
36	43.2	140	168
38	45.6	160	192
40	48	180	216
42	50.4	200	240

There are problems associated with autoleading. Autoleading is self-adjusting. This means it is not fixed—it changes with circumstances. For example, in some programs (especially word processors) placing an inline graphic or large initial cap on the first line of a paragraph can totally screw up the leading, making the line jump away from the rest of the paragraph. This happens because the autoleading for the object is greater than the autoleading for the rest of the paragraph. Sometimes super- and subscripts do the same thing, adjusting leading so that the line where it occurs is spaced farther from the rest of the text—there is more space below or above the line; your page looks unbalanced.

This large initial cap just wrecked havoc with the autoleading in the first line of text, making it leap away from the rest of the text. There is also too much space between the large capital and the body text. We can fix that.

The large initial cap couldn't cause any trouble in this line because the leading was set at a fixed number. The type is 11 points; the leading is 13.2 (120% of the type point size). The smaller text has also been *kerned* closer to the large capital. Kerning will be explained shortly.

To prevent flyaway first lines, always set your leading to a fixed number.

Leading may be heavier if you want an "airy" look to your book. Slightly heavier leading in body text is easier to read than tight leading. Leading set at 130% will accomplish this, but keep in mind that increased leading means increased pages and therefore increased production costs. Heavy leading is another way to pad-out a slim, wimpy book. Avoid leading so wide it looks double-spaced—double-spacing in a typeset book flags you as a publishing imbecile.

This is 12-point type with 14.4-point (120%) leading. It looks balanced, and the ascenders and descenders do not touch each other.

This is 12-point type with 15.6-point (130%) leading. It looks open and airy. The leading is not wide enough to appear double-spaced.

This is 12-point type with 18-point (150%) leading. It looks nearly double-spaced and is reminiscent of the original manuscript. Avoid this blunder.

Tightening leading to less than 110% is not recommended for body text. With leading less than 110%, descenders and ascenders may touch, and the space between them may fill up during printing. Super- and subscripts may also touch letters above or below them if leading is too tight.

This is 12-point type with 13.2-point (110%) leading. It still looks balanced, and the ascenders and descenders do not yet touch each other.

This is 12-point type with 12-point (100%) leading. It looks tight, but the ascenders and descenders still don't quite touch each other. Somewhat risky.

This is 12-point type with 10-point (~80%) leading. It looks cramped, and the ascenders and descenders touch each other. The problem will be especially evident if chemical formulas (NH_4) and exponents (100^2) are present within the text. Annoying to read.

Tightening leading a bit, however, is another way to cheat. You can make type fit by tightening or increasing the leading in just one line or an entire paragraph. Make spare use of this dirty trick—it isn't supposed to be detectable, but often is in unskilled hands.

Word and Sentence Spacing

In typeset books, there is only *one space between sentences,* rather than the two spaces used by typists in word processing. You may have to strip out extra spaces in your manuscript before importing it into a page-layout program. You can globally replace two spaces with one space with your word processor's find/replace feature.

This is a paragraph with short sentences. Two spaces occur after each sentence. This paragraph appears full of holes. Don't do this to your readers. It's not nice.

Once you're ready to typeset your manuscript, you can control word spacing in the page-layout program to keep type tight and readable. There is nothing so distracting as reading a book in which three words are spread across a line. There is no reason to allow this.

When setting up your body text style, you can indicate word spacing ranges that will prevent white patches (rivers) in your book. In InDesign, word spacing is controlled by choosing the JUSTIFICATION in

the PARAGRAPH PANEL, and editing your body text style. Set your minimum word spacing to 80%, desired word spacing to 100%, and maximum word spacing to 120%. For most books, this will be sufficient. It is best not to tweak the character-spacing options too much, as the results can be unpredictable.

The word spacing in this paragraph is set at 100% minimum, 170% desired, and 200% maximum. Notice the holey, Swiss-cheese effect of the overall appearance. This paragraph is hard to read because there is too much space between words.

If you find you have lines that wrap improperly or look goofy, you can always highlight the offending line and change the word spacing for *just that line.* Another cheater's shortcut is to place a soft return ([Shift][Enter] in Windows, or [Shift][↵] on the Mac) where you want the line to break. Soft returns are handy because, unlike hard returns, you don't get a new paragraph, just a new line.

Character Spacing: Tracking and Kerning

Character spacing in Postscript type is automatically handled in a part of the font file called a *kerning table.* Kerning and tracking affect the spacing between letter *pairs* to create visually-consistent letter-spacing. This spacing is specific to the font and will maintain a preset ratio no matter what size the font. In general the *i* takes up $^1/_5$ the space of the *m* in proportional type. Because kerning is done in increments of an *em,* the width of the *em* is dependent on the font you use.

On occasion, you may need to change the tracking or kerning of letter pairs to fit type in a tight space, or to prevent it from overcrowding and becoming hard to read. Always kern for *visual appeal.*

Tracking

You can apply tracking to entire sentences or paragraphs to spread or squeeze type to make it fit a particular space. Access TRACKING through the TYPE menu in InDesign, then choose the CHARACTER option.

Tracking is a percentage of the normal tracking for that font. Compare the word *tracking* in these examples:

Very Loose (+100) ... tracking
Loose (+50) .... tracking
Normal (no added) .... tracking
Tight (-25) .... tracking
Very Tight (-100) .... tracking

Character Width (Horizontal Scale)

You can achieve other letter-spacing effects through changing *horizontal scale* or *character width*. The horizontal scale of the type on the "Part" pages and chapter titles in this book have been adjusted for design reasons. Compare the word *width* in these examples:

50%	width
60%	width
70%	width
80%	width
90%	width
100% (normal)	width
110%	width
120%	width
130%	width
140%	width
150%	width
160%	width
170%	width
180%	width
190%	width
200%	width

Kerning

Manual kerning is necessary when two letters or numbers are too far apart or too close together. Too much letter spacing is commonly encountered in large headlines; the characters may appear unevenly spaced.

The direction of stroke affects how character pairs look. Character pairs with vertical strokes are often too close together. In the example below, the first pair is uncorrected; the second pair is kerned:

IL
IL

Character pairs with curved strokes often appear too far apart. In the example below, the first pair is uncorrected; the second pair is kerned:

PO
PO

Verticals next to curves can touch. In the example below, the first pair is uncorrected; the second pair is kerned:

LO
LO

Super- and subscripted characters tend to print too closely to the previous character. If left that way, these characters may close up and appear muddy when offset-printed or photocopied.

Unkerned:	H_2O	17^2
Kerned:	H_2O	17^2

You can push characters apart (loosen the spacing) or bring them together (tighten the spacing) by placing your cursor between the two offending characters and kerning them in or out. Access kerning through the METRICS option in InDesign, found in the CHARACTER PANEL (Ctrl T) under the TYPE menu. You will have several choices between -100 and +200 to visually correct character pairs. A more precise method of kerning-by-eyeball is use of Alt ← or → in Windows; OPTION ← or → for Mac.

Tabs

Use tabs to position text other that flush left or centered. *Never, ever* use the spacebar to position text—this works only on a typewriter with a monospaced font; it does *not* work in typesetting. With proportional type, spaces are not always the same size—they are the size of the kerning of the character preceding them. The space is wider after an *m* and thinner after an *i*.

Tabs are not things, they are *places*. They mark positions in a line and should be set specifically to a single position. I've had manuscripts come to me with dozens of tabs in them that I've had to remove before typesetting. *Do not* just keep hitting the tab key until the text is where you want it. Highlight the text and set *one tab* for it at the position you want.

In page-layout (and many word processing) programs, tabs come in four types: flush left, center, flush right, and decimal. Make sure you use the correct *kind* of tab or you'll spend many frustrating hours trying to figure out why nothing looks right.

Columns of numbers should always be tabbed with the decimal tab; text never should. Observe what happens with the wrong tabs:

text	tabbed with	decimal tab
12.6	13.2	47.09
297.33	11.4	9888.35

(numerals align properly at decimal point)

text	properly	tabbed
numbers	tabbed	wrong
.345	67.32	911.05
7.71	550.94	68.75

(numerals *do not* align properly at decimal point)

A nasty surprise is awaiting you using right-align tabs with dot leaders following sub- or superscripts, bold, and italic type: Dot leaders will sub- or superscript after a sub- or superscript character. You can correct this problem by adding a space after the sub- or superscript, highlighting the space *and* the dot leader, and removing the sub- or superscript command. Likewise with bolded or italic text. If you don't want that to happen, add a space before the dot leader and remove the style. Tedious, but worth the effort.

Bold Type

Bold type is for headings and subheadings only. Bold type should *almost* never be used in the body text of a book. The only exception is in textbooks or lab manuals, where new terms must stand out. Use of bold type makes your book look like it's been blasted with buckshot, and therefore marks you as an amateur.

This paragraph has **emphasis** indicated with **bold type.** It looks as though it's been **shot** or has some kind of **disease. Never** use **bold** type within **body text**—unless **your book** is a **technical** manual or **educational** text.

Italic Type

Never use underlining in typeset material to emphasize text—use *italics*. Use italics to emphasize, rather than using quotes (as in *example* rather than "example"), to highlight large bodies of creative work—names of books, films, symphonies, and poems—and to denote unnaturalized foreign words. Parts of large creative works—chapters in books, acts in films or plays, and songs—are simply enclosed in quotes, rather than italicized. Avoid overuse of italics, as in long passages or paragraphs (fiction may break this rule).

Italics lean away from what comes before them, creating a gap. So, the space before italicized words should also be italicized. Also italicize any punctuation immediately following italicized words.

Small Caps

Use small caps for table headings, and abbreviations and acronyms such as AM, PM, NASA, SIMM, and CTRL F. Small caps are more readable in serif rather than sans serif type. For table headings, small caps also look best when bolded. Keep in mind that when text is mixed upper- and lowercase, applying small caps will conserve the height ratio of the letters—the capitals will look larger than non-capitals, even though they are all small caps. Most text to be later defined as small caps should be entered in lowercase.

ALL UPPERCASE
BOTH UPPER- AND LOWERCASE
ALL LOWERCASE

Bullets and Numbering

Never use asterisks (*) to bullet lists—use typographer's bullets (Alt 8 in InDesign). Bullets are a nice typesetting feature that help a list of items stand out from the rest of the text. Set items in a bulleted list with a *hanging indent* that allows text to wrap below the previous text, rather than below the bullet or number. Hanging indents are actually *negative* indents. Indent the first line ⅛" (.125") to ⅓" (.34") from the rest of the text, so that the first line is flush left and hangs out from the text following. Simply insert the bullet and press Tab.

> • This line is improperly typeset because it has a bullet without a hanging indent. The text wraps to the next line right underneath the bullet, instead of underneath the previous line of text.
>
> • This text is properly typeset. The wrapping text aligns beneath the previous line because of the hanging indent, and the bullet hangs flush left.

Not all typefaces will produce the same size bullet. Bullets in Times New Roman are larger than bullets in Palatino, and smaller than bullets in Garamond. Once you've made a bullet, you may decide you'd like it smaller or larger. Change the size of one bullet, copy it (Ctrl C—Windows; ⌘ C—Mac), and insert or replace the bullet by pasting it (Ctrl V—Windows; ⌘ V—Mac) wherever you need it.

There are lots of other shapes besides round bullets, available in *dingbat* fonts such as Zapf dingbats, Wingdings, Expert dingbats, to name a few.

ZAPF DINGBATS

A	B	C	D	E	F	G	H	I	J	K	L	M	N	O
✡	✢	✣	✤	✥	✦	✧	★	☆	✪	✫	✬	✭	✮	✯
P	Q	R	S	T	U	V	W	X	Y	Z				
✰	✱	✲	✳	✴	✵	✶	✷	✸	✹	✺				
a	b	c	d	e	f	g	h	i	j	k	l	m	n	o
❀	❂	✼	❅	❄	✽	❉	✾	❃	❇	❈	●	○	■	□
p	q	r	s	t	u	v	w	x	y	z				
❐	❑	❒	▲	▼	◆	❖	◗	❘	❙	❚				

EXPERT DINGBATS

A	B	C	D	E	F	G	H	I	J	K	L	M	N	O
©	©	®	®	™	™	●	●	•	○	○	○	■	■	▪
P	Q	R	S	T	U	V	W	X	Y	Z				
□	□	▫	►	◄	▲	▼	★	♣	♠	♥				
a	b	c	d	e	f	g	h	i	j	k	l	m	n	o
☜	⅛	⅜	⅝	⅞	⅓	⅔	✎	→	←	↑	↓	⇒	⇐	⇓
p	q	r	s	t	u	v	w	x	y	z				
⇑	☒	☑	∅	ⅲ	♈	☂	✓	✓	✄	✄				

WINGDINGS

A	B	C	D	E	F	G	H	I	J	K	L	M	N	O
✌	✌	☞	☜	☞	☜	☝	☟	✋	☺	☺	☹	☣	☠	⚑
P	Q	R	S	T	U	V	W	X	Y	Z				
⚐	✈	☀	❄	❋	✞	✝	☥	✙	✠	☪				
a	b	c	d	e	f	g	h	i	j	k	l	m	n	o
♋	♌	♍	♎	♏	♐	♑	♒	♓	♉	&	●	○	■	□
p	q	r	s	t	u	v	w	x	y	z				
□	❑	❒	◆	◆	◆	❖	◆	☒	◿	⌘				

InDesign's BULLETED & NUMBERED LISTS feature under the TYPE menu is a nifty time-saver for creating nice bulleted and numbered lists with hanging indents. It is not meant to be used with a style; set up your style separately with bulleting or numbering as part of the style. Place bullets by hand with the keyboard command Alt 8 in both Windows and Mac (the Alt key is usually called OPTION on the Macintosh.); numbers are simply entered as usual.

Numbering lists past 9 items poses a particular problem. The numbers have to be right-aligned, rather than aligned flush-left. How do you right-align numbers *and* create a hanging indent? Easy. Increase the indent a squeak, then set a decimal tab *before* the hanging indent. The numbers will align at the decimal.

> 8. This item
> 9. This other item
> 10. This item looks goofy
>
> 8. This item
> 9. This other item
> 10. Perfect alignment at the decimal

Just Say "Ah": White Space

White space is the area on the page that has nothing on it. It is at least as important as the type and graphics. You can achieve design and balance through the proper use of white space, lending a pleasing, uncluttered look to your page. White space makes things easier to read, lets the reader know when one section has ended and another begins, and "chunks out" the page into small digestible, nonthreatening "eye bites." If pages look too crowded and nonstop, book browsers are hesitant to purchase.

Advertising people have known for many years the value of white space. People don't like to read as much as they used to. They are impatient and have less time than in previous years. The ideal brochure for such people is high-impact, *emotive*, sixth-grade-level writing, placed in several small chunks on the page that can be read quickly—"eye-bites."

Bookmaking is following the same trend for the same reasons. Keep your book in small chunks with lots of *functional* (not gratuitous or wasteful) white space and you have a book that those impatient, hurried, and harried readers will feel comfortable with and buy.

Balance, Widows and Orphans

Balance pertains to not only judicious use of white space, but to how the pages align at the bottom margin. Left and right pages should be as even at the bottom as possible. Industry standard says that text must not extend more than 6 points below the bottom margin (not even that, if your printer margin tolerances won't allow it). This is sometimes nearly impossible. There are ways to cheat.

First of all, avoid *widows* and *orphans*. This is not a plea to become cheap and callous, but to watch out for stray text. A widow is less than seven characters printed on the last line of a paragraph, or the first line of a paragraph printed at the bottom of the page or column. An orphan is the last line of a paragraph printed at the top of the following page or column. Both of these typographic creatures look bad and tend to confuse the reader, especially if they occur in narrow columns.

It is best to keep the last line of a paragraph *with* the paragraph and start new paragraphs at the top of the next page. This will sometimes crowd the page past the bottom margin, or leave extra white space at the bottom of a page. What to do?

While an extra line of white at the bottom of a page is rarely a disaster, too much text frequently is. PageMaker allows us to do sneaky things to get pages to break and line up how they should, in which case you're going to have to tweak offending pages by hand.

You may fuss with the leading and word spacing as previously described. You may also select the page with the pointer tool and do some magic. If the last line of a paragraph just squeaks over the bottom margin, you can get it inside the margin by moving the whole page slightly up, making the page squeak over the top margin. If you set up your book per the specs in "Part 2—The Page," you will have plenty of room to do this. No one will notice—it seems that people tend to notice the bottom of the page more than the top.

You can also pull the handles of the inside margin a bit inwards so the text has a slightly larger space in which to flow. No one will notice that the gutter is a tiny bit smaller on one page than the other—this is likely to happen during binding anyway (at least with *basic* and *good* quality printing and binding).

By far a superior copyfitting technique is a *rewrite*. This is the technique used at large publishing houses and it should be yours too. Since it's your book, or you've been put in editorial charge of someone else's book, this is the best option. Cutting a few words, or adding some others (as long as the meaning and intent are not altered), can do wonders for your book. You will be the envy of every wanna-be self-publisher.

Rivers

Rivers are disgusting little apparitions that show up just as you hand the finished printouts to the pressman. They are long willowy strips of white that appear on pages when words conspire against you and line up in strange patterns. This happens when the space between words exceeds the space between the lines. You can see rivers when looking at the page as a whole, rather than the words. Try squinting while holding the page upside-down at arm's length. If you see a snaky strip of white flowing vertically down the page, you have a river. If you see small ponds of white, this is due to poor word spacing.

The only way to correct these watery disasters is to make the words get out of formation. You may add soft returns on tight lines (forced word wrap), or you may have to tweak the tracking or word spacing on a line or two to get rid of the pattern. Also consider a rewrite.

"Hyphenitis"

Hyphenitis is a disease—plain and simple. The only symptom is a succession of hyphens at the ends of several lines on a page. Hyphenitis makes your eyeballs do the mambo in your head, stuttering in their sockets. The page is miserable to read. *Turn off the hyphens.* Automatic hyphens are useful for narrow columns to keep words from spacing bizarrely and wrapping inconsistently, but in half-page or full-page books they are a pain in the asterisk.

The ultimate hyphenation transgression is to hyphenate words *across pages*. "The man was ex-" How would you fill in the missing suffix? Is he *ex*pired? *Ex*communicated? You don't find out until the next page that he was *ex*hausted. You want your readers hanging on your every word—not *half* a word.

A serious case of hyphenitis:

We, the people of the United States, in order to form a more perfect Union, establish justice, ensure domestic tranquility, provide for the common defense, promote the general welfare, and secure the blessings of liberty to ourselves and our posterity do ordain and establish this Constitution for the United States of America.

Headings and Subheadings

Headings are best set in a font different from the body text—sans serif looks cleanest. Your goal is *contrast*. Lower- and uppercase characters are easier to read than all caps. Unless an article *(the, a)*, conjunction *(and, with)*, or preposition *(in, over)* is the first word, it is *not* capitalized in a heading.

Headings and some subheadings should be set larger than the body text—this makes them stand out and easy to find. Headings and subheadings serve to separate your book into smaller sections that make it comfy and inviting to those hurried and harried readers mentioned before. A typical book may have 2–5 levels of headings and subheadings, each set in a different size, and even a different style. The A Head is usually the chapter title; the B Head the first subheading; the C Head the sub-subheading, etc. Typeset C Heads, D Heads, and Table Headers in serif type, as sans serif type is harder to read the smaller it gets.

The leading usually needs to be reduced in multi-line headings:

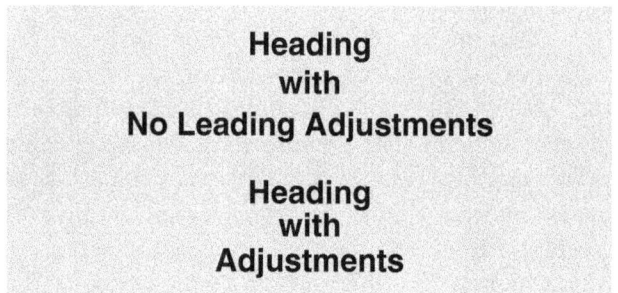

**Heading
with
No Leading Adjustments**

**Heading
with
Adjustments**

If you do use all caps for your heading and the heading is more than one line, the leading should be tightened considerably because there are no descenders on the characters to fill up the space.

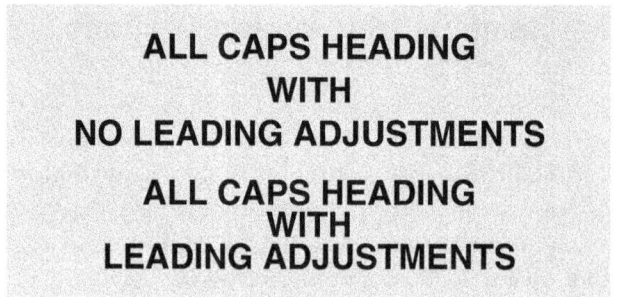

**ALL CAPS HEADING
WITH
NO LEADING ADJUSTMENTS**

**ALL CAPS HEADING
WITH
LEADING ADJUSTMENTS**

Never hyphenate headings. The results may be absurd:

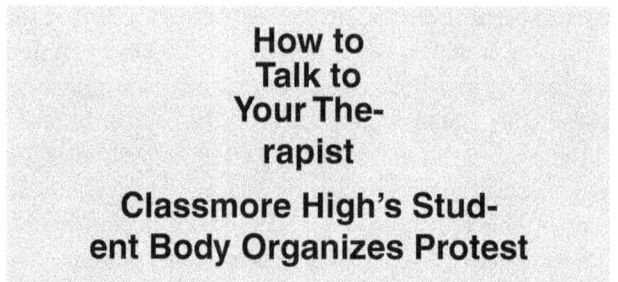

**How to
Talk to
Your The-
rapist**

**Classmore High's Stud-
ent Body Organizes Protest**

Break long headings into logical phrases:

BAD	GOOD
How to Live on $3.00 a Day Anywhere in the U.S.	**How to Live on $3.00 a Day Anywhere in the U.S.**

Mark your manuscript for typesetting. A single box indicates the A Head, two boxes the B Head, etc.

☐ A Head—Chapter Title
☐☐ B Subhead
☐☐☐ C Subhead
☐☐☐☐ D Subhead

Callouts: Parts of a Book

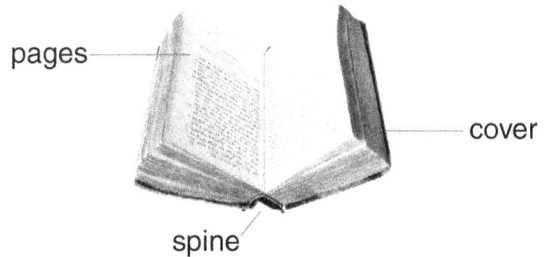

pages

cover

spine

Headings Table

HEADING	ALIGNMENT	STYLE	CASE	FAMILY	SIZE
A Head	centered	bold	all caps	sans serif	125–200% of body text
B Head	centered	bold	normal	sans serif	100–150% of body text
C Head	left	bold	normal	serif	100% of body text
D Head	left	bold italic	normal	serif	100% of body text
Table Header	left, tabs	bold	small caps	serif	80–100% of body text

Captions

Captions are the blurbs below photos and artwork. Center them if they are short, or set the margins to align justified with the borders of the artwork if the caption is longer than one line. Captions are typically two points smaller than the body text.

This is a nicely centered and typeset caption. It is flush with the sides of the box.

Callouts

Those little floating labels in a diagram are called *callouts*. To prevent them from being confused with body text, use a sans serif type. They should be the same size throughout the book—either the same size as or slightly smaller than body text. Bold them only if the letters do not close up with offset or photocopy printing.

Reverse Type

Reverse type (white type on a dark background) is tricky to typeset. Small type fills with ink and closes characters. If you must use reverse type, use bold and increase the point size. If you can't increase the point size, then increase the tracking or width so the letters are spread farther apart.

- Reversed sans serif type—no adjustments
- **Reversed and bolded**
- **Reversed, bolded, tracking very loose**
- **Reversed, bold, tracking very loose, width 130%**
- **As above, in 14 points**

Paragraph Rules vs. Underlining

As mentioned before, *never* use underlining in typeset material. If your book heading or other item needs some kind of line, use a *paragraph rule*. Underlining runs right through character descenders; paragraph rules sit properly just below descenders. You can even adjust the weight and tint of the rule, and indent it slightly from the edge of the text to give your text a purposefully non-underlined look. Paragraph rules work best on headers, table headers, and titles; do not use them within body text.

The descenders in underlined text get run-through.

Paragraph rules look classy and purposefully designed.

Newspaper Columns

Newspaper columns are not uncommon in large 8½" x 11" books. Make sure these columns are *balanced*—the baselines of the lines in one column are even with the baselines of the other column. In InDesign, you can check column balance by placing a *guide*. The example below demonstrates what can happen to columns of text if they are not typeset correctly.

UNBALANCED COLUMNS		BALANCED COLUMNS	
Lorem ipsum dolor sit amet, consectetuer adipiscing elit, sed diam nonummy nibh euismod tincidunt ut laoreet dolore magna aliquam erat volutpat. Ut wisi enim ad minim veniam, quis nostrud exerci tation ullamcorper suscipit lobortis nisl ut aliquip ex ea commodo consequat. Duis autem vel eum iriure dolor in hendrerit in vulputate velit esse molestie consequat, vel illum dolore eu feugiat nulla facilisis at vero eros et accumsan et iusto odio dignissim qui blandit praesent luptatum zzril delenit augue duis dolore te feugait nulla facilisi. Lorem ipsum dolor sit amet, consectetuer adipiscing	elit, sed diam nonummy nibh euismod tincidunt ut laoreet dolore magna aliquam erat volutpat. Ut wisi enim ad minim veniam, quis nostrud exerci tation ullamcorper suscipit lobortis nisl ut aliquip ex ea commodo consequat. Duis autem vel eum iriure dolor in hendrerit in vulputate velit esse molestie consequat, vel illum dolore eu feugiat nulla facilisis at vero eros et accumsan et iusto odio dignissim qui blandit praesent luptatum zzril delenit augue duis dolore te feugait nulla facilisi. Nam liber tempor cum soluta nobis eleifend option congue nihil imperdiet doming id quod mazim placerat facer possim assum. Lorem ipsum dolor sit amet,	Lorem ipsum dolor sit amet, consectetuer adipiscing elit, sed diam nonummy nibh euismod tincidunt ut laoreet dolore magna aliquam erat volutpat. Ut wisi enim ad minim veniam, quis nostrud exerci tation ullamcorper suscipit lobortis nisl ut aliquip ex ea commodo consequat. Duis autem vel eum iriure dolor in hendrerit in vulputate velit esse molestie consequat, vel illum dolore eu feugiat nulla facilisis at vero eros et accumsan et iusto odio dignissim qui blandit praesent luptatum zzril delenit augue duis dolore te feugait nulla facilisi. Lorem ipsum dolor sit amet, consectetuer adipiscing elit, sed diam nonummy nibh euismod tincidunt ut laoreet dolore magna aliquam erat volutpat. Ut wisi enim ad minim veniam, quis nostrud exerci tation ullamcorper suscipit	lobortis nisl ut aliquip ex ea commodo consequat. Duis autem vel eum iriure dolor in hendrerit in vulputate velit esse molestie consequat, vel illum dolore eu feugiat nulla facilisis at vero eros et accumsan et iusto odio dignissim qui blandit praesent luptatum zzril delenit augue duis dolore te feugait nulla facilisi. Nam liber tempor cum soluta nobis eleifend option congue nihil imperdiet doming id quod mazim placerat facer possim assum. Lorem ipsum dolor sit amet, consectetuer adipiscing elit, sed diam nonummy nibh euismod tincidunt ut laoreet dolore magna aliquam erat volutpat. Ut wisi enim ad minim veniam, quis nostrud exerci tation ullamcorper suscipit lobortis nisl ut aliquip ex ea commodo consequat. Lorem ipsum dolor sit amet.

river

poor word spacing

baselines uneven

Typographer's Characters

Here comes the juicy part. Typographer's characters make the difference between a professionally typeset book worthy of respect, and a novice's lubberly hack-job deserving of a dumpster.

Quotes vs. Inch Marks

Typographer's quotes are to foot and inch marks what Dom Perignon® is to Budweiser®. I can't count how many times I've seen inch and foot marks used in place of proper quotes and apostrophes. This is by far the most common blunder in creating an attractive, professional-looking book.

What you get when you type direct from the keyboard is a foot mark for an apostrophe (') and an inch mark for double quotes ("). Typographer's quotes are sometimes *curly*—depending on the font—but are always thicker on the bottom for initial quotes ("), and thicker at the top for ending quotes ("). The same rule applies to single quotes (quotes within quotes). Apostrophes are merely an ending single quote.

Typewriter foot and inch marks are the dead giveaway of a nonprofessional. InDesign and most other layout programs automatically convert foot and inch marks to typographer's quotes during import. If you will *not* be using a layout program to make your book (you'll be toughing it out in your word processor), you can set the options or preferences (see your manual) in your word processor to produce "curly quotes" or you can type in typographer's quotes from the keyboard using ASCII codes.

		Windows	Mac
"	Opening Double-Quotes	Alt 0147	Option [
"	Closing Double Quotes	Alt 0148	Option shift [
'	Opening Single Quote	Alt 0145	Option]
'	Closing Single Quote (Apostrophe)	Alt 0146	Option shift]

(Expanded lists of ASCII and Mac keyboard codes are found later in this chapter.)

Em Dashes

The *em*-dash (called a "mutt" in printer's lingo) is used as a sharp pause, and for parenthetical passages. InDesign will automatically covert two hyphens (without spaces before or after) into a typographer's em-dash while importing text from your word processor.

You can type an em-dash directly into any program with the ASCII code Alt 0151 typed from the numeric keypad.

> Stop - don't set an *em*-dash like this...
>
> ...or with an *en*-dash – like this!
>
> Don't do this either--it's for manuscripts only.
>
> This is right—see?

En Dashes

Use an *en* dash ("nut") for number ranges, phrases with *to* in them, and words with hyphenated phrases. Examples are 15–25, toe–to–toe, and anti–blood-clotting.

> Don't set number ranges like this: 15-25
> Use an *en*-dash, as in 25–36

Page-layout programs such as InDesign incorporate special key combinations that produce em- and en-dashes, or type en-dashes in Windows directly from the numeric keypad with the ASCII code Alt 0150.

Superscripts and Subscripts

Most modern word processors automatically change certain text to super- or subscripted text, but this feature must be enabled (consult your manual).

Super- and subscripts should be about 60–70% of the body text point size. If you use the auto super- and subscript commands in your word processor without resizing them by hand, InDesign will properly import and resize them into your layout.

If you do not have automatic super- and subscripting enabled in your word processor, you will have to resize super- and subscripts individually—or globally with the *search and replace* function if your word processor allows it. (In Word, you can tell the *search and replace* command to look for all super- and subscripts of a particular size and replace them with super- and subscripts of another size.)

You can also set the super- and subscript size and positions in most layout programs. You can do this for the entire program or just for a particular style. Set the size to 60%, superscript position to 30%, and subscript position to 10–20%. For hand-built fractions (something you'll have to get used to in some page-layout programs) the subscript position should be 0 (zero) so the subscript is even with the baseline.

Not Typeset	Typeset
NH_3	NH_3
17^2	17^2
1/8	$\frac{1}{8}$

Fractions

Three fractions are available through ASCII codes in Windows: ¼ (Alt 0 1 8 8), ½ (Alt 0 1 8 9), and ¾ (Alt 0 1 9 0). These will serve you well. Use ASCII codes only if these three fractions are all you will ever need in your book.

But what if you need ⅙ or ⁸⁄₉? In InDesign (and many other page-layout as well as word processing programs) you will have to *build them*. If you have unusual fractions (i.e., *not just* ¼, ½, or ¾) in the same book, *do not* use ASCII-code-generated fractions. They will not match the ones you will have to create. In this case, it's best to create them all by hand. The good news is, once

you make one, you can put it on the pasteboard in your page-layout program (or in the clipboard, or stored as a spike, in the glossary, or as a macro in word processors) so you can use it again, changing the numbers only. This way you don't have to meticulously typeset each and every fraction.

Type out the fraction, as in 1/6, then typeset the numerator as superscript (60% size, position 30%), and the denominator as subscript (60% size, position 0%). Do nothing to the divider bar (or use Option Shift 1 on the Mac for a typographer's fraction divider bar). You now have a fraction—⅙.

All hand made fractions will probably have to be manually kerned, as the super- and subscripts sit too far from the divider bar. Observe:

Unkerned:	¹/₂
Kerned:	½

Thin Spaces

The thin space is a useful and little known type-tweaking device. Access it with the command Alt Shift Ctrl M. Thin spaces are ⅓ of an em and are used to move em dashes slightly away from the text, or to put a little space between single quotes within double quotes. Use of the thin space in these circumstances is entirely up to you and your design sensibilities.

> ***Without*** **Thin Spaces:**
> —page 12—
> she went—no, she *split.*
> Cathy said, "Georgio thinks I'm a 'real card'"
>
> ***With*** **Thin Spaces:**
> —page 12—
> she left —no, she *split.*
> Cathy said, "Georgio thinks I'm a 'real card'"

Do *not* use thin spaces in place of kerning, as the space is bigger than a kerned space and inaccurate compared to precision kerning.

In addition to thin spaces, many other kinds of spaces are available in InDesign (under the Type menu, Insert White Space option) and other page-layout programs, such as hair space, sixth space, third space, etc.

Styles

The most efficient way to format type is to set up and use *styles*. Styles allow you to ensure consistency across several different files making up a book. You will never have to remember any of the attributes you set for your book if you let the styles remember for you.

Once you set up a style, you can apply it over and over again to different sections of text, instantly formatting that text as body text, chapter heading, subheading, callout, or any other part. Indents, tabs, leading, point size, type style, and white space will all be remembered and applied in the blink of an eye—without having to apply these things one at a time. Best of all, should you change your mind about, say, the point size of the body text, all you have to change is the *style*, not all of the text where the style is applied. Once the style is changed, all the text with that style changes automatically. Instant typesetting!

Page-layout and advanced word processing programs are wizards at styles. You can set up styles in a template that you use over and over again for each chapter, *and* you can copy styles from one file to another.

If you set up a style sheet and modify the styles in your book template *before* importing your manuscript into your page-layout program, typesetting your book will be a breeze.

Your goal in creating an attractive and readable book is *contrast*. Light, delicate serif type should contrast with assertive and strong sans serif type. Never use two sans serif fonts close together—there isn't enough contrast between them. The same holds true for serif fonts.

Special Characters

In Windows, you can access special characters through ASCII codes ([Alt] plus numbers from the numeric key pad) and through keyboard combinations on the Macintosh.

Note: Not all special characters are accessible with all fonts. Times and Times New Roman have the most extended set of characters available. Fonts such as Bodoni and Microstile, for example, are missing some special characters from their character sets—such as em-dashes. You must insert these using another font. Plan ahead! An ASCII code table is found on the next page.

A Typical Style Sheet for a Book

	BODY	A HEAD	B HEAD	C HEAD	TABLE	CAPTION	CALLOUTS
Font	garmnd	helv	helv	garmnd	garmnd	garmnd	helv
Size	11	18	14	12	12	10	10
Type Style	normal	bold	bold	bold italic	bold sm caps	italic	bold
Leading	13.2	21.6	16.8	14.4	14.4	12	12
Word Spacing:							
Minimum	80%	80%	80%	80%	80%	80%	80%
Desired	100%	100%	100%	100%	100%	100%	100%
Maximum	120%	120%	120%	120%	120%	120%	120%
Alignment	justify	center	center	left	left	justify	center
Hyphens	off	off	off	off	off	off	off
Indents	.25"	n/a	n/a	n/a	n/a	n/a	n/a
Tabs	.25", .5"	n/a	n/a	n/a	.25", .5", .75", 1"	n/a	n/a
White Space:							
Before	0	0	1"	.25"	.2"	0	0
After	0	2"	.5"	.15"	.1"	0	0

ASCII Codes for Special Characters (Windows Only)

Alt Code	Character	Alt Code	Character
0124	|	0198	Æ
0133	…	0199	Ç
0134	†	0200	È
0135	‡	0201	É
0136	^	0202	Ê
0137	‰	0203	Ë
0138	Š	0204	Ì
0139	‹	0205	Í
0140	Œ	0206	Î
0141		0207	Ï
0145	'	0208	Ð
0146	'	0209	Ñ
0147	"	0210	Ò
0148	"	0211	Ó
0149	•	0212	Ô
0150	–	0213	Õ
0151	—	0214	Ö
0152	~	0215	×
0153	™	0216	Ø
0154	š	0217	Ù
0155	›	0218	Ú
0156	œ	0219	Û
0159	Ÿ	0220	Ü
0161	¡	0221	Ý
0162	¢	0222	Þ
0163	£	0223	ß
0164	¤	0224	à
0165	¥	0225	á
0166	¦	0226	â
0167	§	0227	ã
0168	¨	0228	ä
0169	©	0229	å
0170	ª	0230	æ
0171	«	0231	ç
0172	¬	0232	è
0174	®	0233	é
0175	¯	0234	ê
0176	°	0235	ë
0177	±	0236	ì
0178	²	0237	í
0179	³	0238	î
0180	´	0239	ï
0181	µ	0240	ð
0182	¶	0241	ñ
0183	·	0242	ò

Alt Code	Character	Alt Code	Character
0184	¸	0243	ó
0185	¹	0244	ô
0186	º	0245	õ
0187	»	0246	ö
0188	¼	0247	÷
0189	½	0248	ø
0190	¾	0249	ù
0191	¿	0250	ú
0192	À	0251	û
0193	Á	0252	ü
0194	Â	0253	ý
0195	Ã	0254	þ
0196	Ä	0255	ÿ
0197	Å		

Macintosh Special Characters

Key Combination	Character
Option E	é
Option U	ü
Option N	ñ
Option I	î
Option C	ç
Option Shift C	Ç
Option 1	¡
Option 3	¿
Option ;	…
Option Shift 8	•
Option $	¢
Option Shift 5	ligature of fi
Option Shift 6	ligature of fl
Option Shift 1	/
Option [	"
Option Shift [	"
Option]	'
Option Shift]	'

Part 6

Artsy Stuff: Graphics

Hairpulling: Computer Graphics

Paste-Up and Other Archaic Activities

Paste-up? We don' do no stinking paste-up!

We have computers. We can measure, trim, crop, edit, resize, color-correct, and paste graphics into our documents electronically. We never have to go near a skinny knife, a pasteboard, a glue pot, a T-square, or a light-table ever again. Computers have replaced the archaic tools of yesteryear with simple commands often having the same names as their outdated counterparts (cut, paste, crop, resize, adjust color balance, etc.). All is available at the click of a mouse button—*if* you don't go insane learning how to do it.

An Expedition Through Computer Graphics Hell

One of the best ways to get graphics—drawings, paintings, or photos—into your book is to *scan* them in with a computer peripheral that converts images into 0s (zeros) and 1s (ones), to be stored and manipulated on your computer.

How a Scanner Works

The scanner uses a CCD array (charge-coupled device, for you *technerds* out there) to capture images. It bounces light off the image, detecting how much light reflects back. The scanner then converts this information into digital form for storage in the computer's RAM. Scanner software is used to manipulate the values of the stored image.

The scanner does not actually *see* black and white—it sees shades of gray. However, when sampling the image, the scanner must decide whether a dot is black (on), or white (off). The result is a digitized scan stored as black and white at differing *bit-depths*—convincingly faking grays.

Scanner Calibration

Calibrate your scanner before using it right out of the box. Calibration compensates for differences between monitor, scanner, and printer to get consistent results. Without proper calibration, grays may print as black or much lighter than you would expect, and the problems can be profound when working with color.

Some scanners include a test file that when printed, will automatically calibrate your scanner to print the proper shades of color and gray on your printer. Use it. Other programs, such as CorelDraw and Adobe Photoshop, also have automatic calibration routines built into the programs. You might also consider making yourself a "tint sheet" that shows how your printer reproduces grays at 5% or 10% increments. The higher the dpi of which your printer is capable, the finer the distinction between grays, and the smaller percent change required to visually notice the distinction.

Graphic File Formats

Scans are always bitmaps—an array of pixels at a set resolution (described later), regardless of file type. TIFF files are the most versatile scan file type because they are transferable across many computer platforms. This means that they can be read by DOS-based, Macintosh, and Amiga (dinosaur alert!) computers. Best of all, they are *transparent*—they do not have to be converted or translated (as many other files do) to be read by different computers or imagesetters (providing they are not compressed). The TIFF file format is the preferred scan format within the publishing industry. Other common bitmap file types include Windows bitmaps (.bmp) and jpegs (.jpg).

Resolution

Resolution is the term for the number of dots or lines crammed into a square inch of area. Resolution is measured in two ways: *Optical resolution* refers to the maximum number of dots the scanner can *see*; *logical resolution* is the maximum number of dots the scanner can *interpolate* (in-TER-po-late) to increase effective resolution.

Setting correct resolution is important not only in considering quality, but for practical file size. Higher-resolution scans eat up disk space—some can't even fit on a 100-MB Zip disk; lower-resolution scans are sometimes less clear. The trick is finding the happy medium that prints at a lower resolution than your printer's maximum (thereby letting the printer interpolate a reduced file size), while maintaining crisp quality output. This is no easy task. To make matters more confounding, lower-resolution scans frequently look better than graphics scanned for the maximum resolution of your printer. *Hi-res isn't always the best quality.*

300-dpi scan (864 KB)

200-dpi scan (339 KB)

An uncomplicated rule-of-thumb in scanning technology is to scan color and grayscale graphics at 200–266 dpi (dots per inch). Surprisingly for 600 dpi laser printers, the best output for grayscale may be closer to 200 dpi, as the printer interpolates the "missing" pixels: There is frequently no visible difference between 200 and 600 dpi on some printers, and the file size is *much* smaller.

In the printing industry, newspapers use graphics of 60–85 dpi; magazines 120–133 dpi; and books use 150–266 dpi resolution. The effective resolution of your graphics is oftentimes determined by the *quality of the paper* on which you print. Rough, low-grade paper (newsprint) allows ink to spread, making the dots run together and darkening the image. High-grade glossy paper lets ink spread less, and the images are sharper and lighter. Color scans always look best at a somewhat higher resolution than grayscale, printed on coated glossy stock. Color printers typically print at 360 to 2880 dpi—beware: file size of color scans can be huge!

Graphics may be *dithered* at either the scanner or the printer. Dithering is the term used to describe how computers combine dots of several colors or grays, and blend them to create another color. For example, cyan, magenta, and yellow dots are dithered to create brown. Experiment with the settings in the printer and the scanner to see which device dithers the best, then dither only from the scanner *or* the printer. *Dithering* is also used interchangeably with halftoning.

If your printer does halftoning (and most modern printers do this exceptionally well), *do not* halftone your scan—this, in effect, will result in *double*-halftoning when it is printed. The results can be unpredictable and ugly. Scan such artwork as "photo" or "grayscale."

Grayscale saves gray values as a *depth* of gray because the scanner maps grayscale as *bit-depth*, which translates to dot size at the printer (deep = a large dot; shallow = a small dot).

Adjusting brightness and contrast in grayscale scans is an exercise in trade-offs. If you increase brightness to get more detail in light areas, you will lose light grays. If you increase contrast to emphasize differences among grays, you will lose light and dark details. Decreasing contrast emphasizes light and dark, but washes out mid-tones.

The easiest way to adjust grayscale scans is to adjust the gamma or levels. You'll want a few white dots in black areas, and a few black dots in white areas. Print a proof, then set the scan back to grayscale before saving it to disk.

If you want to halftone your photos for special purposes, have fun experimenting. Normal halftoning has more grays, but fewer details; fine and extra-fine halftoning will result in more details, but fewer grays.

For black and white (ink) drawings, scan with "line art" selected in your scanning program. Line art looks best scanned at 600–2400 dpi, but the file size may be prohibitive. Stick with 600 dpi and the quality won't suffer too much. File size can still get pretty big—perhaps up to 10,000K (10 Mb) for a full 8½" by 11" page.

Set the brightness while zoomed in: Thin lines should almost disappear, closely-spaced lines should be distinct and separate. Darken slightly so thin lines revert from a string of dots to a line.

Common Printer/Imagesetter Resolutions

OUTPUT DEVICE	DPI	FINAL OUTPUT QUALITY
typical dot matrix (9-pin)	27	draft
typical typewriter (cloth/ink ribbon)	90	draft
NLQ—near letter quality (9-pin dot matrix, daisy wheel typewriter)	180	draft
LQ—letter quality (24-pin dot matrix, some ink jets)	360	photocopies
laser, ink jet	300	photocopies, basic offset
laser, ink jet	600	basic to good offset
color ink jet	720	good offset
premium color inkjet	1440–2880	premium offset
Imagesetter, high-end laser	1200	good offset
Imagesetter	1270	good offset
Imagesetter	2400	premium offset
Linotronic	2540	showcase offset

Screen Frequency (Ruling)

Screen ruling is dependent on the number of dots in your scan. A 4" x 5" image scanned at 150 dpi has 450,000 dots—a bunch. For most purposes, screen ruling is set at half the dpi, and what follows may be safely ignored.

Halftones are continuous-tone images converted to dots (look at a newspaper photo with a magnifying glass to confirm this). The dots in a halftone are boxes. Screen frequency determines how many boxes will be grouped together to form a *halftone cell,* which determines how many lines are in a screen. (Dithering affects the number of halftone dots per cell.) The cell, in turn, determines the size of the halftone dot. For example, a 150-lpi halftone screen has 150 halftone cells, or dots per inch.

Divide the final resolution of your output device by lines per inch in the screen, and you know how many dots are in each halftone cell.

> 300 dpi ÷ 100 lpi = 3 dots per halftone cell
>
> 600 dpi ÷ 150 lpi = 4 dots per halftone cell
>
> 2540 (linotronic) ÷ 133 lpi = 19 (rounded off) dots per halftone cell
>
> 2540 (linotronic) ÷ 225 lpi = 11 (rounded off) dots per halftone cell.

Screen ruling also affects the number of shades of gray that will be printed. The fewer lines in your screen, the more grays you will print. The more lines, the fewer grays. Apply this formula:

$$(\text{Resolution} \div \text{screen ruling})^2 + 1 = \text{number of shades of gray}$$

EXAMPLES:

$(300 \text{ dpi} \div 200 \text{ lpi})^2 + 1 =$	3 shades of gray
$(300 \text{ dpi} \div 100 \text{ lpi})^2 + 1 =$	10 shades of gray
$(300 \text{ dpi} \div 85 \text{ lpi})^2 + 1 =$	13 shades of gray
$(600 \text{ dpi} \div 200 \text{ lpi})^2 + 1 =$	10 shades of gray
$(600 \text{ dpi} \div 100 \text{ lpi})^2 + 1 =$	37 shades of gray
$(600 \text{ dpi} \div 85 \text{ lpi})^2 + 1 =$	51 shades of gray
$(1200 \text{ dpi} \div 150 \text{ lpi})^2 + 1 =$	65 shades of gray
$(2540 \text{ dpi} \div 150 \text{ lpi})^2 + 1 =$	288 shades of gray

(the eye can see only 256 shades of gray)

Scan Ratio

Scan ratio is the ratio between scan resolution and screen ruling. For example the scan ratio of a 600-dpi graphic screened at 300 dpi is 600:300, or 2:1. If the scan ratio is <1:1, *pixilation* occurs (block-steps). No improvement in quality occurs in a scan ratio greater than 2:1.

Scan ratio uses mathematical formulas for scanning an image for both optimum quality and file size. There will be times when you will want to scan an image at a different size from the original. Scanning at a smaller size will reduce file size. The scan can then be resized in your document.

The rule for figuring scan ratio is: Divide the original scan dpi by the reduction/enlargement factor. (Initial resolution ÷ sizing factor = effective resolution.)

Decide how big the scan needs to be in your document *before* you scan it, then do the math and scan it at the proper size.

For example, to scan an 8" x 10" image that will print at 4" x 5", scan it at 100% at 150 dpi, then resize. The printout will be 50% size at 300 dpi.

To scan a 4" x 5" image to be printed at 8" x 10", scan at 600 dpi and resize. Printout will be 200% at 300 dpi.

In the above examples, everything comes out just fine. But, what happens if you scan an image at 150 dpi, and later need to enlarge it? Bad news. A 150-dpi scan enlarged 200% will print out at 75 dpi—newspaper resolution—and certainly not good enough for your book.

Screen Angle

The angle at which colors are printed determines how the eye sees color. The *screen angle* is the angle of the cells. The screen angle of a halftone determines how well colors and shades are *blended*.

Black and white photos should have about a 45° screen angle. This setting is usually the default for most printers and software, as wide variations can produce unpredictable results.

Color separations are arranged in a rosette pattern with a screen angle of 45° to 105°. (K = 45°, M = 75°, Y = 90°, and C = 105° are common standards.)

If not adjusted properly, *moiré* patterns (weird plaid, herringbone, or bull's eye interference designs) will result. PostScript Printer Definition (PPD) files automatically adjust screen angles so you don't have to mess and guess with them. Inkjet printers do not require special settings, as they are set at optimum for most uses.

Scaling

Going nuts trying to figure out what to type in the resizing box in your scanner or paint program? If you type 25% in the resizing box, what size will it *really* it be? Don't forget, graphics resize in *two* dimensions—horizontal and vertical. We may know that 25% is ¼, but the graphic will actually be ⅛ the original size if you reduce it to 25%.

PERCENT/MAGNIFICATION TABLE	
400% = 8x	100% = 1x
200% = 4x	75% = 0.5x (½)
175% = 3.5x	50% = 0.25x (¼)
150% = 3x	25% = 0.125x (⅛)
125% = 2.5x	12.5% = 0.0625 (¹⁄₁₆)

Never manually rescale a halftoned scan; moiré patterns will result.

Bits, Bytes, and Gasps

Computer graphics are stored—as are all computer files—as *bits* of information. Eight bits equal one *byte*; 1024 bytes equal one *kilobyte* (K); a thousand kilobytes is a *megabyte* (MB).

Computer graphics come in 1-bit, 4-bit, 8-bit, 24-bit, 32-bit, 36-bit, and 48-bit size:

1-bit	Black and white line art
4-bit	16 colors or grayscale
8-bit	256 colors or grayscale (indexed color)
24-bit	16,777,216 colors: 8 bits for each of 3 colors—cyan, magenta, yellow—CMY for print; or RGB—red-green-blue—for screen display
32-bit	billions of colors (8 bits for each of 4 inks—cyan, magenta, yellow, black—CMYK)

*higher resolutions include color-matching information used in special publishing applications

Since there are *three bytes* per dot in a 24-bit color graphic, the number of dots in the graphic multiplied times three bytes equals the file size. The file size can get out of hand quickly.

And now for your surprise...

Do you think you need a 4800-dpi 32-bit color scanner? The following table will make you think again.

Computer Graphics Table

Resolution	Colors	Size per inch²	File Size for 4" x 6" Image
72	1-bit	0.7K	16.8K
72	4-bit	2.8K	67.2K
72	8-bit	5.6K	134.4K
72	24-bit	16.8K	403.2K
150	1-bit	2.8K	67.2K
150	4-bit	11.2K	268.8K
150	8-bit	22.4K	537.6K
150	24-bit	67.2K	1.6MB
300	1-bit	11.2K	268.8K
300	4-bit	44.8K	1.07MB
300	8-bit	89.6K	2.15MB
300	24-bit	268.8K	6.45MB
600	1-bit	44.8K	1.08MB
600	4-bit	179.2K	4.3MB
600	8-bit	358.4K	8.6MB
600	24-bit	1.75MB	25.8MB
1200	1-bit	179.2K	4.3MB
1200	4-bit	716.8K	17.2MB
1200	8-bit	1.43MB	34.4MB
1200	24-bit	4.3MB	103.2MB
2400	1-bit	716.8K	17.2MB
2400	4-bit	2.87MB	68.8MB
2400	8-bit	5.73MB	137.6MB
2400	24-bit	17.2MB	412.8MB

Obviously, by the time we have gazed at the bottom of this table, our eyeballs have switched sockets—perhaps more than once.

A 413-meg graphic? Well, so much for the *extra-spiffy-ooh-ah* scanner—you don't need one. Anything over a 24-bit graphic scanned at 600 dpi, for most applications and desktop systems, is unusable. Leave the 4800-dpi, 32-bit color scanners to the people who make coffee table books. Chances are, that's not you.

Memory and File-Size Management

Graphics can be memory hogs. If your computer has less than 2 GB of RAM and your printer isn't tricked out with extra RAM, you may need to think about speeding up potentially glacial-speed processing. What do you have a fancy 'puter for, anyway—to watch it slog along like a Commodore-64 during a brownout? No! Screen redraw or printout in a geological time-span won't make your day.

Here's what you can do:

- Upgrade or add a graphics card. Even adding more VRAM (if possible) to your current card will help.

- Display the graphics *placeholders* or wire-frames, in your layout program, rather than the whole graphic. This greatly speeds up screen redraw. Or, set your program to display graphics in lower resolution; this will help speed up page scrolling. Unfortunately for Adobe PhotoShop users, the reverse actually happens: PhotoShop holds *two* complete copies of every graphic in memory while you work on it, so that you may "revert" quickly to a previously-saved version.

- Link your graphics in your layout program, rather than imbed them. However, linked graphics *must* be present where layout programs can find them when you need to print.

- Rotate or crop scans in a photo manipulation or paint program *before* placing them in your document. This saves your page-layout program from having to recalculate the coordinates each and every time it prints (in which images are rotated/cropped at the printer), therefore saving memory in both the printer *and* the computer. This also saves lots of thumb-twiddling.

- If you must resize scans, do so in a photo manipulation or paint program. Otherwise, your page-layout program has to do it. Again, this takes memory and wastes time.

- Do not leave EPS or WMF graphics ungrouped. Always group these graphics and make them one unit before you print, otherwise the printer will moan along trying to calculate each and every node in the path. EPS files with many nested groups will also slow printout. Sometimes, these will not print at all if your printer memory is feeble.

Other Computer Graphics Formats

Many graphics formats are available. Though TIFFs (the publisher's universal file format) are preferred for publications, other graphics are useful.

Other bitmaps are created by most paint programs. These include BMP, PCX, and GIF formats. The PCX format is considered a DOS-based computer graphic; GIFs are best suited to web-based displays. Don't forget: Bitmaps become jagged and boxy with enlargement.

- Jpeg—Joint Photographic Experts Group (JPG) files are very popular for both screen-based applications such as e-mail and web design, and print. Jpegs are squeezed with a "lossy" compression to decrease file size. This "lossy" compression strips data from the file during saves to make the file smaller, so jpeg graphics must be handled with care to prevent degradation of quality.

  It is best to save jpegs as tiffs before you do any editing of them, otherwise each time you save the file it becomes more and more degraded. Edit and resave the tiff file to your heart's content.

  When your graphic is exactly as you want it and you will be doing no more editing, it may then be saved as a jpeg to reduce file size and save disk space. When saving jpegs for print, save them with the least amount of compression to insure highest print quality. If you want the very best quality your printer can produce, do not use jpegs at all for print media, but only for screen-based applications.

- Windows metafiles (WMF) are vector-based graphics with very smooth lines created by *bezier curves*. Windows metafiles are created in drawing programs, rather than paint programs. These graphics are completely scalable and maintain their smooth lines at *any* size.

- Mac PICT files are the Macintosh version of a Windows metafile. They are a vector-based graphic and are scalable.

- Computer Graphics Metafiles (CGM) are also vector graphics. CGM graphics are the universal form of vector graphics.

- Encapsulated PostScript—EPS graphics are an industry-standard vector graphic composed of bitmap graphics that have been smoothed with PostScript code. They will not print properly—if at all—on non-PostScript printers. Encapsulated PostScript files are scalable.

File Conversions

Graphics files can be converted into each other with the proper software and/or filters. Most scan software allows you to save graphics in a variety of formats. Cross-platform conversions are no longer an issue. The only thing to remember is that service bureaus with Linotronic output need EPS files.

Quick Tip

Writing Guidelines for Nonfiction:

- Derive arguments from facts on the page—not the ones left in your head!
- Personalize the narrative to draw the reader inside your mind and heart.
- Always keep in mind that everything you say must *mean* something to the reader, have some kind of personal significance.
- Seduce your readers' acquiescence with a compelling argument:
  - **Thesis-driven:** isolated bits of evidence to prove hypothesis
  - **Data-driven:** totality of data leads to inevitable conclusion
- **Chapter Development:**
  - *Narrative*—who's relating the story: you, me, someone else?
  - *Break* the facts and exposition, alternating, for example, with a discussion of research findings with historical perspectives, or a quote from an authority, as in, "According to Dr. Salk..."
- **The Argument:**
  - *Present* the facts—funnel the data
  - *Interpret* the facts—must be invulnerable to attack
  - *Relate* new concepts to familiar ones
  - *Elicit* sympathy by presenting competing interpretations
  - *Persuade* towards the conclusion—show the data as irrefutably supportive
  - *Express* the implications—the argument stems from facts and rational speculation, not the reverse

Part 7

Color
Separations

Going Totally Bald: Color Separations

What's a *Separation?*

Color photos cannot be printed as is at a printing press, or even through your home inkjet printer. The colors you see in the most complex photograph will be created by combining only four ink colors: cyan, magenta, yellow, and black. A professional printing press needs to make plates of each of these colors from color separations. Colors must be *separated* into the four components and printed out on individual sheets from your printer with black ink where the colors will go. These separations are then made into film and printing plates, and are eventually recombined to print the all of the colors in your original photograph.

All About Color

You will probably want one or more colors (in addition to black and white) for your book cover. A working knowledge of how color is handled by the computer compared to the colors we see in light, is essential to becoming proficient in preparing color separations for the printing press.

Colors are of two types: additive or subtractive. *Additive* color is *light*. Light is what you see on the screen (red, green, and blue light pixels—RGB). Additive color is all white when all colors are present (as in sunlight), and all black when no colors are present. Additive color is counter-intuitive: 100% red plus 100% green makes yellow.

Subtractive color is the color in *ink*. When white light (all additive colors) strikes an ink, light reflects from that ink *unequally*, imparting the particular color of the ink that we see. The colors we don't see are absorbed by the ink—*subtracted*—from the white light. The subtractive primary colors are cyan, magenta, and yellow (CMY). These three colors are created by subtracting the additive primaries from white light.

White - red	=	cyan
White - green	=	magenta
White - blue	=	yellow

Complementary colors are colors that when combined, make white. Red and cyan, green and magenta, and blue and yellow all make white when paired.

SUBTRACTIVE PRIMARY	ADDITIVE PRIMARY
cyan	green and blue
magenta	blue and red
yellow	red and green

ADDITIVE PRIMARY	SUBTRACTIVE PRIMARY
red	magenta and yellow
green	yellow and cyan
blue	cyan and magenta

Monitor colors may or may not match printed output because the color you see is light—additive color. The monitor cannot accurately display 100% cyan, for instance. Colors are affected by monitor control knobs, monitor age, and ambient light. Many color printer can print to match screen colors.

Spot Color vs. Process Color

Spot color is opaque and comes pre-mixed in the container. This makes it less expensive than process color, if you need fewer than three colors. Spot colors can be printed on top of other colors (especially process colors) without creating a new color from the mixture. A *tint* is a gradation (percentage) of the base color and can be printed on the same separation—and the same plate—as the base color (i.e., green and light green). Tints can be printed from your computer in 1% increments, but printing presses are capable of only 5% increments. Spot colors can be edited in imported EPS graphics; process colors cannot.

Process color differs from spot color. Process color is translucent—light passes through the inks so that complementary colors are absorbed (wiped out). Printing colors on top of other colors will mix them and change the colors to a new color. This is why we need to *knockout* and *trap* the colors (no, we aren't hunting possum). These techniques are described shortly.

Process colors are known as CMYK: C = cyan, M = magenta, Y = yellow, and K = black. All of the colors in nature can be printed by blending these colors in different percentages. K is necessary because CMY cannot produce a true black; it is actually a very dark brown. Mixing the CMYK colors with a Pantone matching system (PMS) is called *color build* in printing.

Only process (CMYK) or spot colors can be printed. If you've used RGB to set up your file, all of these colors will have to be converted to process or spot colors before you print your separations for the press.

Common Color Matching Systems

System	Color Type
Crayon	
DIC® Color Guide	spot and process
FOCALTONE®	process
Greys	spot and process
MUNSELL® High Chrome	
MUNSELL® Book of Color	
PANTONE® coated	
PANTONE® ProSim	
PANTONE® uncoated	
PANTONE® process	spot and process
PANTONE® process Euro	spot and process
TOYO®PC	spot
TRUMATCH 4-Color Separations	process

Printing Complications

There's more to color printing than meets the eye. The more colors you use, and the closer those colors are to each other, the more tweaking you'll have to do to get them to behave. Clean *color-breaks* in your colors are your goal.

Stalking the Elusive Clean Color-Break: Knock-Outs and Trapping

Knocking out process colors prevents their mixing. Say, for instance, you'd like to print yellow letters over a red background. Overprinting would result in orange letters—not what you had in mind. So, you *knock out* the color in the background (creating precisely-shaped white cutouts for the letters), and the letters will print yellow.

Trapping is the procedure that allows you to make the knockout larger or smaller, so the objects fit together correctly and don't leave any unsightly white gaps (the registration of the printing press governs how much gap occurs).

Trapping creates a *spread* or a *choke*. If the object on the top is lighter than the object underneath (as in our yellow letters on red), make the object slightly *larger* than the knockout, so it will *spread* a tiny bit (a hairline-width) over into the red.

If the object on the top is darker than the color beneath it (such as red letters on a yellow background), put a *choke* on the knockout by making it a tiny bit *smaller* than the object.

Manual trapping is a bit complicated. The border around the object to be knocked-out and trapped should overlap the object by .125" (⅛"). Use a hairline width with no fill. Make sure you use process, rather than spot colors. The color of the line should be a new third color that combines the highest CMYK values from the original colors of the object and the background. Bring the line to front in your arrangement of layers.

To print color separations in most layout programs, access the print dialog box, then simply check the separations option or check the box "print this ink" for each color listed.

CMY color model   **RGB color model**

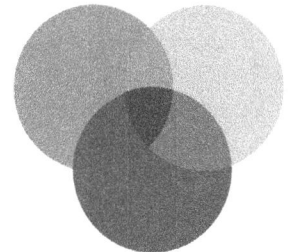

Color and Printing Presses

Before you do color separations on your computer, ask your commercial printer what color-matching systems they use, and which one they prefer. Also find out if they want you to include printer's marks on your mechanicals. These include color ramps, calibration bars, registration marks, crop marks, and other information. Also find out if you should print these marks inside or outside the margins on your separations.

Printer's Marks:	color ramps, calibration bars (density-control), registration marks, crop marks, separation color (C, M, Y, or K). Increase margins: .75" vertical, .75" horizontal
Page Info:	file name, page, date. Increase margins: .50" vertical, 0" horizontal
For both:	Increase vertical margins by .875"; horizontal margins by .75".

Film

You can save money by printing the film yourself. Film may be either positive or negative, and printed emulsion-side up, or emulsion-side down. (The emulsion side is the side treated with chemicals.) Check the *mirror* box in the print dialog box to print emulsion-side down.

Some commercial printers prefer that you not attempt color separations from your computer—especially color photos. They want the originals.

Don't argue. Just give them what they need. Your project comes before your ego.

A special device called a *raster image processor* (RIP) is used to convert pre-press from computers to a format imagesetters can understand.

A last-minute color change in a line drawing or text (such as black to green) is called *drop-in color*. Standard drop-in colors are cyan, magenta, yellow, green, and purple. Any other colors will have to be mixed.

Original artwork is of two types. *Reflective art* is opaque photos, paintings, and drawings. *Transparent art* is slides. Be sure to ask your printing press what kind of art they want.

In a standard print order, colors are specified by writing 4/0—meaning 4 colors on one side of the page, no printing on the back; 4/1—4 colors and one on the back; 4/2—four colors and two; 4/4 ("four over")—4 colors on both front and back pages.

Ink Coverage

The highest possible ink coverage is 400% (100% each of CMYK). Since this can create mud at the press, colors have to be adjusted so that total ink coverage (TIC) does not exceed certain limits. The ink coverage should not exceed 250–320%; 250% for uncoated paper, and 320% for glossy stock. TIC is best close to 100%; this decreases drying time of the printed sheets so imprints of them won't end up on the back sides of the next sheets off the press.

To control how much ink gets on the paper, you will be employing mathematical techniques called *Under Color Removal* (UCR) or *Gray Component Replacement* (GCR). GCR is used for one color; UCR is used for an entire publication. These techniques replace equal amounts of CMY components with K (black). Believe it or not, this won't visibly change the colors.

Say you have a color separation with values of 60% C, 70% M, 50% Y, and 20% K. These values added together = 200%. We can get the total ink coverage down to 100% by subtracting 50% from every value of CMY, and adding 50% to K. Thus, you will have 10% C, 20% M, 0% Y, and 70% K. You've cut your ink coverage in half (50% of 200% = 100%).

Black ink doesn't have to be printed at 100% saturation. The *black limit* should be 75–80% on uncoated paper; 85% on coated.

Dot Gain

Dot gain is the tendency of ink to spread on the paper (a paper with good *ink holdout* will minimize this effect). Dot gain is acceptable up to 22% on matte stock; 20% on glossy stock.

Printer's Gradient Ramp to check press ability to print tints and shades

Lines will get thicker with most printing methods due to dot gain. When using lines (as in lines, boxes, and ovals—LBOs—in the toolbox of most layout programs) choose a *line weight* (thickness) one increment smaller than what you want.

Using the hairline weight is a bit tricky. A hairline width is .25 of a point, or the best resolution of the computer printer you are using. Hairlines will also get thicker with most printing presses and photocopies, *except* on a 2540-dpi Linotronic—here, they vanish, so use a thicker line. Tinted hairlines will also not print well on Linotronics.

Bleeds

When ink appears to go all the way to the edge of the paper, it's called a *bleed*. The ink is not really printed to the edge—press margins and gripper tolerances prevent this. Bleeds are printed on oversized paper that is later trimmed to your book dimensions. You must add about ⅛" (depending on the printing press) to the outer margins of your pages if you use bleeds in your book.

Crossovers

Text or graphics that spread across from one page to another in a layout are called *crossovers*—they cross over the gutter to the other page. Two pages are printed with half of the material, which are then trimmed and carefully aligned during binding. High-quality presses do this well; don't ask for crossovers from a basic to good hometown press—they can seldom align the pages accurately due to mechanical restrictions. This caveat also applies to electronic printing presses.

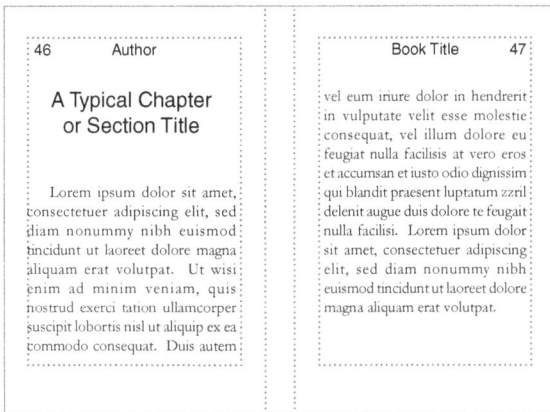

Standard book spread

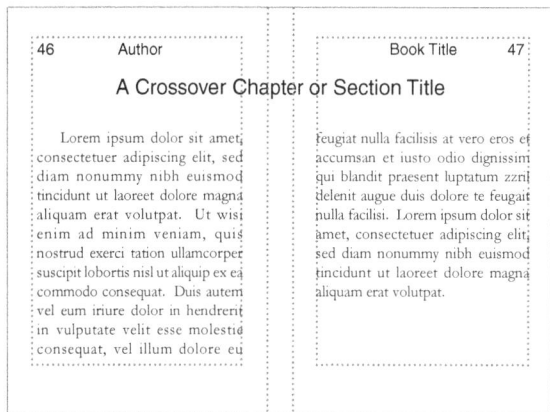

Book spread with crossover

Just for Fun

Back in the beginning, everyone spoke English. Then the Welsh, disliking how things were run, moved to the west side of the island, where they were attacked by the Irish, who stole all the vowels. When the Danes invaded, the Irish gave the vowels to them, telling them they were all pronounced "ooo."

Part 8

Paper

What's to Know About Paper?

The Paper Mill

Paper making is a complex and surprisingly fast process, perfected over centuries. At the modern paper mill, the raw ingredients travel through 400 feet of machinery sending the *furnish* (raw wood pulp and water) over and through a series of wire mesh screens and rollers, traveling nearly a mile in under four minutes. The end product is a 20-foot-wide roll of paper weighing four tons, from which smaller rolls and sheets are cut. An average paper mill can produce 350 tons of paper a day. Paul Bunyan, run for your life.

Paper begins as wood chips and sometimes rags mixed with sulfite or sulfate and water. This mixture is heated and beaten, creating a chemical reaction that separates the mass into pulp. The impurities are removed and then bleach is added.

The pulp is beaten more so the fibers will adhere to each other, then rosin is added to make the fibers slightly water-resistant. Water is added next—about 100 pounds per pound of chemical pulp—and the resultant mash becomes *furnish*.

The furnish pours into a *headbox* where it is taken up on a wire mesh belt called a *fourdrinier*. The fourdrinier lays the furnish flat and shakes gently from side-to-side, draining water and aligning fibers.

The furnish then passes under a *dandy roll* to get a finish imprinted into the surface (laid, wove, felt).

Water jets cut and trim the edges—a high-powered spray gives a clean edge; a lower-powered spray leaves a feathery *deckle* edge.

More and more water is removed as the furnish passes through a succession of heated rollers. After about a mile of winding up and over and between rollers, it is left with only 5% water.

The paper then passes through *calender* rollers that flatten and smooth the paper to varying degrees of texture, thickness, and gloss, according to what kind of paper is desired. It is the degree of calendering (in addition to the finish imparted with the dandy roll) that creates the different kinds of paper available today.

Twenty-five to 40% of the cost of book printing is in the cost of the paper.

Most papers are 10% eucalyptus and 40% recycled wood pulp; the rest is cut forest pine.

Groundwood or mechanical pulp is the lowest grade paper. It contains impurities and is unbleached. Cardboard and newsprint are examples.

A promising paper alternative is *kenaf*, an African okra relative that grows 12 feet in less than 4 months. It yields 3½ times as much cellulose per acre than pine wood per year.

Chemical pulp goes to make free sheets. The impurities are washed away and the pulp is bleached. Bleach increases *whiteness;* titanium is sometimes added to increase *opacity;* acids may be added for waterproofing. (Nonacid paper makes books last much longer, but they are sensitive to water damage.)

There are many grades of chemical-pulp paper. Grade is determined not only by bleaching, pigments, and other additives, but *calendering* that smooths the paper. By passing long webs of still-wet paper pulp through a series of rollers, paper can be smoothed to many gradations. Calendering also alters the opacity, whiteness, bulk, and *ink holdout* of the paper. Bulky papers are very opaque, and have a flat finish because they have been calendered little. Thin papers are less opaque, have better ink holdout, and are usually glossy because they have been *supercalendered*. The most opaque papers are rough, thick, coated, dark, and made from groundwood—standard waxed cardboard, for example. Adding cotton also increases opacity.

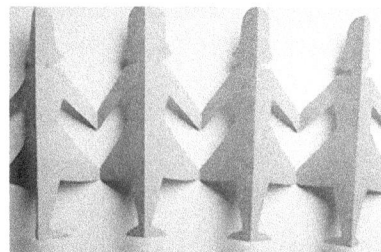

Calendering Table

PASSES	ROLLERS	UNCOATED	COATED	
1	2	vellum	matte	*Less Calendering* more opaque more white more bulk less gloss less smooth less brittle less ink holdout
2	4	antique	dull	
3	6	wove	gloss	*More Calendering* less opaque less white less bulk more gloss more smooth more brittle more ink holdout
4	8	smooth (satin, luster)	ultragloss	

Common Paper Textures

Several paper textures are available for different applications. You may be familiar with the term *bond*. Bond paper is the most common paper type. Bond paper for everyday use is usually all wood pulp.

Bond paper is sold on cotton-content rating: 0%, 25%, 50%, 75%, and 100%. Zero-percent cotton is sulfite paper and is the least expensive; cost goes up with cotton content.

- *Wove* paper is smooth and hot-air textured through puckering (cockled).
- *Laid* paper resembles papyrus. The texture is pressed into the paper with fabric-coated rollers (dandy roll) when it is still 90% water.
- *Felt* paper has the pattern pressed into it while it is still 80% water.
- *Linen* paper has the pattern pressed into it while dry.
- *Offset* paper smoothness is determined by calendering. It is available in several smoothnesses.

Uncoated paper is standard book text paper with a light texture. Printing on deeply textured paper will decrease the sharpness of the type. Characters may fill in, especially reversed type.

Coated paper is coated with minerals (clay) that may crack when folded. Scoring can prevent this. Coated paper provides sharp characters but the increased glare from the surface may cause eye strain.

Cover Stock

Cover stock for perfect-bound books (standard paperback) comes in *calipers* of 8-point, 10-point, and 12-point, or in weights such as 80#, 100#, and 110#.

Covers are specified as coated on one side (C1S) or coated on two sides (C2S). The coating is a smooth, sometimes glossy finish. This coating is part of the processing of the paper and is not the same as varnishing or laminating, discussed in "Part 10—Book Binding."

Magnified Views of Paper Textures

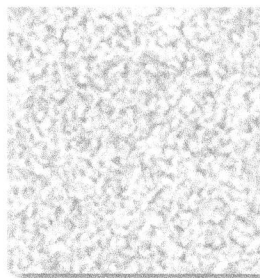

Sulfite Bond

25% Cotton Bond

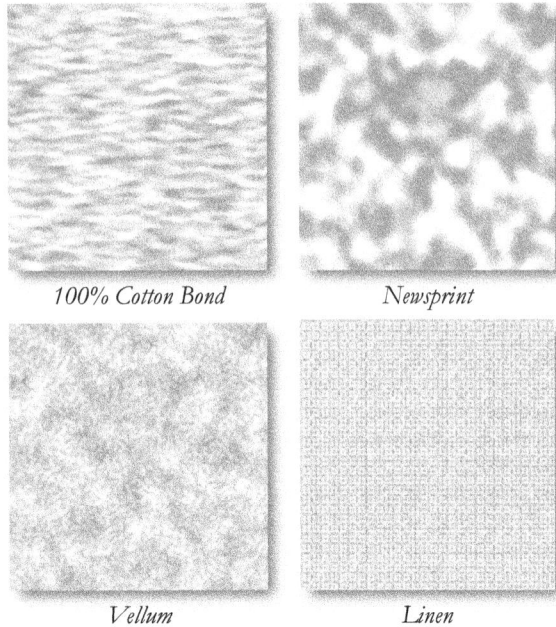

100% Cotton Bond

Newsprint

Vellum

Linen

Paper Grades

Paper is rated #1 for premium, down to #5 for commodity grade.

Paper Grades Table

1	2	3	4	5
Bond	**Text**	**Uncoated Book**	**Coated Book**	**Cover**
20#	24#	50#	magazine	80#
photocopies	70#	60#	catalog	110#
business papers	80#	offset	calendar	cardstock
writing papers	premium textured	publishing	poster	8 pt C1S
communications	tinted fiber	ads	coated offset—	10 pt C1S
premium— print felt side only	laid linen	ink soaks in	wt. ⅔ base, ⅓ coating wt.	12 pt C1S
DP—dual purpose, laser bond	felt deckle edge		good ink holdout vivid color	
for NIP— non-impact printing smooth and clean	ink soaks in			

Paper Grain

Grain is the orientation of the fibers in the sheet relative to its cut. The grain depends on how the paper was cut from the roll out of the paper mill. A *grain long* paper has fibers running its length. A *grain short* paper's fibers run its width (100% cotton bond example, left).

Grain long paper keeps a tighter register in an offset press. Very heavy or very lightweight papers behave best if grain short.

Folds are smoother with the grain rather than against it. Folds are stronger against the grain. Book pages with the grain parallel to the binding turn more easily, lie flat, and don't pucker along the spine.

To determine grain (if it isn't listed on the paper package), tear the sheet both horizontally and vertically. The smoother tear determines the grain, as tears are neater *with* the grain. Wetting the paper also helps determine grain: The paper will curl parallel to the grain.

Paper Size

Paper comes in sheets for *sheet-fed* presses, and rolls for *web* presses. *Cut stock* is standard paper in use every day in laser printers and copy machines. *Parent sheets* are the large sheets on which signatures are printed and folded. Papers measured in metric are usually foreign papers.

Cut Stock: 8½" x 11" and 11" x 17"

Parent Sheets: 23" x 35" (print area is 22" x 35") (allows for grippers and trimming) 25" x 38" (print area is 22" x 35") (allows for bleeds and color ramps)

Bond paper comes in 8½" x 11, 8½" x 14", and 11" x 17", (cut stock sizes) and 17" x 22" (parent-sheet size).

Text (vellum), offset, and coated papers come in 25" x 38" size.

Coverstock comes in 9" x 12" (cut stock) and 20" x 26" (parent sheet).

Paper Weight

Paper weight is measured from the *basis weight*—the weight of a ream (500) of *parent sheets*. Two papers of different sheet-size can weigh the same, but one feels thicker. Papers with irregular basis weights are usually foreign papers.

Paper weights can be confusing. What's the difference between 60# book paper and 24# bond? Nothing.

Paper Weight Conversion Table

40# book paper = 16# bond

50# book paper = 20# bond

60# book paper = 24# bond

90# book paper = 50# cover stock

110# book paper = 60# cover stock

120# book paper = 65# cover stock

130# book paper = 70# cover stock

140# book paper = 75# cover stock

145# book paper = 80# cover stock

175# book paper = 110# cover stock

Paper Weight Uses Table

		UNCOATED	COATED	
BOND	TEXT	BOOK	BOOK	COVER
16#, forms	50–80#	50–70#	60–110#, sheet-fed	60, 80, 100#
20#, photocopies			30–70#, web press	8, 10, 12 pts
24#, stationery				

Paper Caliper

Paper *caliper* (thickness) is measured in points or thousandths of an inch with a *micrometer*. Six points are $^6/_{1000}$". When making books, knowing the caliper of the paper will help you calculate the thickness of the book—and therefore, how large the type should be on the spine when designing the cover.

Common Paper Calipers

PAPER TYPE	INCHES/SHEET	INCHES PER 4-UP SIGNATURE	INCHES PER 8-UP SIGNATURE	PRINTED BOOK PAGES/INCH
25% cotton bond, 24# laid	.0058	.0464	.0928	340
#1 offset, 60# vellum	.0050	.04	.08	400
#2 opaque offset, 60# smooth	.0046	.0368	.0736	432
25% cotton bond, 24# linen	.0045	.036	.072	444
commodity offset, 50# smooth	.0040	.032	.064	500
premium #4, dual-purpose bond	.0039	.0312	.0624	516
ultra-premium #1, coated 90# gloss	.0038	.0304	.0608	532
#1 coated, 80# dull	.0036	.0288	.0576	552
12 pt cover C1S	.012			
10 pt cover C1S	.010			
8 pt cover C1S	.008			

Knowing book thickness will also lead to important information regarding shipping and storage. All of the specifications for a book's dimensions including trim size and spine width are called the *bulk specs*.

When a book needs to be thicker (usually to ensure that spine text prints properly, or to justify a higher cover price), the book is *beefed-up* by using thicker paper.

When a big book needs to be *slimmed down* to reduce shipping costs and shelving problems, use a thin-caliper paper (or a smaller body-text font and deeper margins).

Book Thickness

PAGES	PAPER	THICKNESS
248 pp	60# vellum offset	.65"
248 pp	60# high-bulk offset	.78"
248 pp	60# gloss-coated	.375"
248 pp	60# smooth offset	.575"

Ink Holdout

Coarse and uncoated papers have less *ink holdout* than smooth, coated, and glossy papers. Ink holdout is the tendency of the ink to stay on the surface, rather than soak into the paper. Absorbent paper requires fewer lines in halftone screens (as in newspapers). Ink holdout affects light reflectance: The smoother the paper, the better the ink holdout, the more reflective the paper.

Whiteness

A rough surface increases ink absorption, which decreases brightness because the light becomes scattered in many directions when reflected from the surface.

A smooth surface decreases ink absorption, which increases brightness because light is reflected back evenly.

Brightness

Both opacity and brightness are measured with a *densitometer*. The brightness of paper is determined by its whiteness and its smoothness.

BRIGHTNESS %	PAPER TYPE
near 100	paper with fluorescent dyes
94–97	offset, photocopy
90–95	letterhead, text paper
88–92	standard laser paper
81–88	business forms
75	facial tissue
40	cardboard
20	paper grocery bag

Paper Specs

Purchasing paper or specifying to your printer which paper you prefer, entails writing *paper specs* in an industry-standard shorthand.

First, note the quantity, followed by the size, the grain, the weight, the color, the brand name (if known), the finish, and the grade. A typical paper purchase order might look something like this:

500, 11 X <u>17</u>, 24#, natural, PerfectPaper Corp., linen, #1.

The underlined <u>17</u> in the size specification denotes grain long (underlining the <u>11</u> would indicate grain short).

Paper Suppliers

Beaver Prints	Office Depot	On Paper
305 Main Street	1-800-685-8800	P.O. Box 1365
Bellwood, PA 16617	WWW.OFFICEDEPOT.COM	Elk Grove Village, IL 60009-1365
Paper Access	Paper Direct	Papyrus Place
23 West 18th Street	100 Plaza Drive	2210 Goldsmith Lane
New York, NY 10011	Secaucus, NJ 07094-3606	Louisville, KY 40218
Queblo	Quill Corporation	Staples
1000 Florida Avenue	100 Schelter Road	1-800-333-3330
Hagerstown, MD 21741	Lincolnshire, IL 60069	WWW.STAPLES.COM
Transatlantic Arts, Inc.	Writer's Supply Club	
P.O. Box 6086	P.O. Box 26524	
Albuquerque, NM 87197	Baltimore, MD 21207	

as you would a book. Place paper susceptible to wrinkling or buckling, in the middle of a big stack to keep it flat.

Condition the paper by exposing it to the press room several hours before the print run. Acclimating the paper helps keep a tight register.

Paper Care

Paper is delicate stuff. Temperature and humidity affect *dimensional stability*, the quality of fitness that makes it runnable and printable. *Runnability* describes how well the paper moves through the press; *printability* refers to how well it reproduces the image.

Excessive drying, heat, or moisture will buckle the paper, decreasing runnability.

Very dry paper collects static—disastrous in electrostatic printing, but not so critical for offset printing.

Store paper flat in stacks away from windows, heaters, or direct lamp light. Do not store paper on edge

Lily Splane

English...
The Most Confusing Language

Just for Fun

1) The bandage was *wound* around the *wound.*

2) The farm was used to *produce produce.*

3) The dump was so full that operators had to *refuse* more *refuse.*

4) We must *polish* the *Polish* furniture.

5) He could *lead* if he would get the *lead* out.

6) The soldier decided to *desert* his *dessert* in the *desert.*

7) Since there is no time like the *present,* she thought it was time to *present* the *present.*

8) A *bass* was painted on the head of the *bass* drum.

9) When shot at, the *dove dove* into the bushes.

10) I did not *object* to the *object.*

11) The insurance was *invalid* for the *invalid.*

12) There was a *row* among the oarsmen about how to *row.*

13) They were too *close* to the door to *close* it.

14) The buck *does* funny things when the *does* are present.

15) A seamstress and a *sewer* fell down into a *sewer* line.

16) To help with planting, the farmer taught his *sow* to *sow.*

17) The *wind* was too strong to *wind* the sail.

18) Upon seeing the *tear* in the painting I shed a *tear.*

19) I had to *subject* the *subject* to a series of tests.

20) How can I *intimate* this to my most *intimate* friend?

Part 9

The Printing Press

Ready for the Press

Pre-Press Preparations: One Last Check

If and when things begin to go wrong (with the emphasis on *when*), you will need to know where in the book production roster of duties it has occurred. Did you choose the right font? *Were you brain dead?* Did you *set up* your file for the right printer device? *Were you brain dead?* Did you use type correctly? *Were you brain dead?*

It is possible that at least one out of the above four possibilities will be responsible for your print problems.

Of the print horrors to unfold, several others top the list:

- The page contains not words, but a tangled mass of gibberish. (You tried to print a Postscript file with a Postscript driver on a non-Postscript printer.)

- Characters are closed-up with ink or toner. (Low-grade quality paper; character tracking is too tight; font point-size is too small.)

- The type is smudged as if licked by a beagle. (The paper is slipping on the print rollers; the paper is jamming. Clean the printer. Or, you grabbed a wet page hot off your inkjet printer. Stop that.)

- Type runs together as if afraid of the page. (The tracking got hosed—fix it; your text block might be too narrow—pull the handles with the pointer tool so the type spreads out.)

- Type resembles secret-agent encryption. (You tried to print a Windows file with many imbedded ASCII codes, on a Macintosh, or vice-versa. Macintosh and DOS ASCII are not identical. Some special characters will not print correctly.)

- Your eyeballs sizzle in their sockets while reading. (You're using tiny sans serif type. Knock it off.)

- Your book looks like it was intended for the legally blind. (Big type is not attractive. If you don't have enough wordage to make a decent book, make a booklet.)

- Your book looks like a ransom note. (You've used too many type faces. Isn't it pretty? No, it looks stupid. Stick to two font families—one for body text, the other for various headings.)

- Your book looks like someone shot it at arm's length. (You've committed the amateur's sin of using **boldface type** and ALL CAPS type within body text.)

- Your book looks like a second-grade reader. (Big type with mammoth margins is not attractive to adults. See Jane Novice make a book. See Dick Expert laugh. Shame, shame, Jane.)

Mechanicals

You've been through many proofs by now, shrieking with angst at every misplaced comma, every misaligned tab. The final (yea!) printouts from your computer printer are called *mechanicals*. Ask your printing pressman if he requires registration marks, and if they should be inside or outside of the final book margins. Most page-layout programs can print registration marks and color ramps on each page (within your printer's margin constraints) as your pressman requires.

Mechanicals are sometimes affixed to 10-point card stock for fitting on scanner drums for making plates.

You may place a tissue overlay on the final printout to indicate any special instructions for the page. Your pressman may ask you to provide acetate overlays if you want type printed *on* photographs in your book. This is a very old method of applying type to photos, so it won't be likely to happen.

Include a photocopy dummy (no, not a Xerox® of Dan Quayle) so your pressman will know what you have in mind as a final.

Stages of Press-Proofs

Bluelines are simply positive contact sheets. You may or may not get these to check over. Sometimes printing presses charge extra for them; bypass this stage if that's the case.

The final proofs for the book-to-be are called *repro-proofs*; these are made with cameras from your mechanicals. Imagesetters work by *photocomposition*—exposing film with all characters on a grid, whereby only the characters desired actually develop. It's an elimination process. The repro-proofs are used to make the plates that will be put on the press to print pages.

The *cover-mechanical* is the mock-up for the cover design. It is a collection of acetate overlays, usually assembled on a paste board or light table. The Big Guys still do it the old-fashioned way—we don't have to. Our results on computer can be just as impressive as those produced in the soon-to-be-obsolete way.

The *press proof* is the printed cover without the text (jacket blurbs) on the back. The press proof sells the book and is put in catalogs, ads, and shown to bookstore managers. Guess what? As far as marketing books is concerned, you *can* tell a book by its cover, because that's how bookstores buy them—by the cover!

You may sometimes find tiny flaws (missing period, extra comma, etc.) in the repro-proofs. Rather than printing a whole new set of mechanicals with the corrections and delaying the print-run another week or two, large publishing firms often advocate a nasty little trick called *patching*. Patching is a—hopefully—soon-to-be-dead practice. Patching entails pasting corrections to a repro-proof from a duplicate set of proofs. We've all seen magazines and newspapers in which it looks as if someone has just jammed in a block of type. It's obvious. If you care about the quality of your book, fix the problem at the source and print out a new page. With computers, things happen faster than they used to—there won't be the 1–2 week delay that large houses suffer.

Printing Methods

There are generally two acceptable and inexpensive methods of producing many copies of your book: electrostatic (photocopies), and offset ink printing.

Electrostatic: Laser and Photocopy Technology

Though offset printing is superior in quality to most photocopies, photocopied books can be of good enough quality for selling books by direct mail and in specialty shops. *Tip:* If you don't have a duplexing printer that prints on both side of the paper at the same time, print mechanicals for photocopies back-to-back on high-quality paper. Print even pages in order, reinsert them in the paper tray (take care to position the pages correctly, paying attention to the direction of the header, and whether pages need to be face up or face down), and print odd pages on the backs in reverse order. This is to prevent the people at the copy shop from making a master set of copies for their duplexing copier, and copying from the copies—creating instant mud. Luckily, photocopiers these days can also print from PDF files, so you'll just need a disk or jump drive.

The advantage to photocopies is that you can print as few copies as you like. The cost is frequently reduced for print-runs of 100 or more. Above 500 copies, offset printing is usually less expensive than photocopies. The disadvantage of photocopies is that most high-speed copiers reproduce documents at only about 60 dpi—photograph and halftone scan quality will degrade significantly. Also, the toner has a tendency to scuff and flake off, especially if printed on heavy paper.

How Electrostatic Printing Works

1. Light flashes on the original—recording the image.
2. The image passes to a mirror and is reflected through a lens and shutter to another mirror.
3. Light strikes a moving plastic belt (copy machine) or a drum (laser printer) and electrostatically charges the belt or drum with the image.
4. The belt or drum is dusted with toner powder that sticks to the charged areas.
5. The paper contacts the belt or drum, transferring the image.
6. The image is bonded to the paper by passing the paper through heated rollers.

Keep in mind that some distributors and upscale bookstores will not accept photocopied books. They may actually sniff the books for the piquant scent of petroleum-based ink.

Offset Ink Printing

There are two basic types of offset printing presses: sheet-fed and web. Sheet-fed presses take pre-cut sheets and print an imposition of pages in *signatures,* which are then folded and gathered with other signatures, and trimmed and bound into a book. The Perfecter sheet-fed press prints both sides of a sheet at once.

The web offset press prints on a roll of continuous paper ("web" refers to the paper), and the sheets are cut after each signature. Newspapers usually run on web presses.

The Cameron press is a web press that prints in 12-page signatures. The plates have direct contact with the paper. This press also folds, trims, and binds the signatures into perfect-bound or case-bound books. The advantage of a Cameron press is its speed and inexpensive print-run; the disadvantage is that this press can print in only one color.

Ink

Printing ink is petroleum-based (unless you specify expensive soy-based ink) and is transparent. The underlying paper color affects the color of the print.

Though opaque ink is available, it usually requires two passes. This is called *double-bumping.*

Ink is like thick honey or molasses. This quality is called *tack.* The press has water fountains that thin the ink and clean the plates with each pass, preventing gummy ink buildup.

To get an idea of how the ink works on the paper you have chosen, ask for a *drawdown.* If the printer is willing to work with you, there should be no charge for this press check.

Varnish for book covers costs the same as another color. Presses usually charge a wash-up fee for every color other than black, including varnish.

How a Sheet-Fed Offset Press Works

The offset printing process is called *offset* printing because the image is *set off* in reverse onto a rubber-coated roller called a *blanket cylinder.* The offset press transfers images from the blanket cylinder, rather than directly from the plates (as in a Cameron press). This saves wear on plates, and insures a tight contact with the paper. Plates are right-reading, and transfer the inked image to the rubber blanket wrong-reading, which then transfers to the paper right-reading.

The standard offset press embodies a chain of devices and parts that each do a specific job. Offset presses are large or small (small presses are sometimes called *duplicators*).

1. At the top of the press are the *ink fountains,* having *ink-flow adjustment keys.* Small presses have 1 fountain with 10–12 keys; large presses have 8 fountains with 50–60 ink-flow keys.

2. Next are the *ink transfer rollers.* Small presses have 4–5 rollers; large presses have 18–20 rollers.

3. Then comes the *water fountain.* The water fountain contains *dampening solution*—a mixture of water, acids, gum arabic, and alcohol.

4. Next is the *plate cylinder* where the actual *photographic plates* ride.

5. Then is the *blanket cylinder,* where ink is transferred from the plates.

6. The *paper feed* is next. *Grippers* grasp the paper and feed it into the press where the blanket makes an inky impression. The gripper tolerance on small presses is $3/8$" minimum. No margin should measure less than this in your final printout for making plates. Most large presses can handle $1/4$" margins.

7. The *registration unit* hugs the paper and keeps it in position so that the pages print exactly aligned, no matter how many passes (colors) the sheets must be run through. The more expensive the press (and therefore the printing job), the higher the quality of print and the more accurate the registration of the pages.

8. Once gripped and hugged, the paper goes around the *impression cylinder,* gets sent down the *delivery chain,* gets grabbed by the *delivery grippers,* and ends up in the *delivery paper stack.* All done!

Any miscalculations on the pressman's part—improper key adjustments in ink and water fountains, press misalignment—will result in a crummy print job. Dropped-out halftones indicate that there isn't enough ink flowing. Plugged-up halftones indicate too much ink is coming through. Printing, as you see, is a precision science. The pressman's know-how, as well as his investment in equipment, is why printing costs so much.

> **Tacky ink** can make rough or lower-grade paper *pick*. Loose fibers from *picking* can accumulate on the press and cause *piling* and uneven ink coverage in printing.
>
> As a rule of thumb, solids larger than 3" x 3" don't print well on small presses. Small presses provide less-precise ink coverage. See the "Print Quality Variations Table" on page 105 for details.

Print Problems

PROBLEM	PROBABLE CAUSE
Banding	low spot on a worn blanket
Doubling	slight second contact with blanket—roller pressure poor
Excessive Dot Gain	too-coarse paper, too-high blanket or cylinder pressure
Hickies	dust sticking, making white donuts on black solids
Mottling	poor ink transfer (too-coarse paper, misaligned cylinders, worn blanket)
Setoff	wet previous page left imprint
Slurring	side slippage, poor blanket pressure or ink tack.
Smudges	handling prints while wet
Streaks	worn gear or ink roller
Tracking	exit wheels got inked
Uneven Ink Density	poor blanket or cylinder pressure; ink piling
Waviness	web-pull on web press—nearly unavoidable
Wrinkles	paper-weight too light

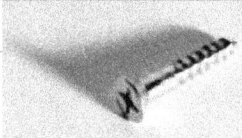

"Buddying Up" To Your Printer

You can't go wrong by making friends with your pressman. Take time to appreciate his job, don't ask for rush jobs or special considerations, and he'll be a loyal partner throughout your publishing life.

Printing presses are busy places; they wouldn't stay in business long if they weren't. What keeps them busy is lots of customers. Recognize you are not his only customer—there are probably many customers ahead of you in the printing queue.

Ask questions if you don't understand something. Press people are simultaneously bored and harried—they like to explain things and show you how everything works, but only if not pressured. There's a joke in the press industry that goes like this: If your pressman (the guy who actually runs the press) has been at the same place for more than six months, he's probably lost his mind. Watching sheet after sheet of paper zip through a press is akin to watching grass grow.

Printing Industry Customs

The printing industry—like the publishing industry—conforms to a set of protocols of which the uninitiated need to be aware. Minor policies may vary from press to press, but you'd better watch out for the biggies.

1. Quotes not accepted and acted on within 60 days (sometimes fewer) are subject to review.

2. Orders cannot be cancelled once underway.

3. Experimental work performed at the customer's request cannot be used until the printer is paid in full.

4. Creative work supplied by the printer remains the property of the printer until the customer pays for it.

5. Condition of copy received must be as good as described. It must be clean copy or the quotation becomes void.

6. Negatives and plates belong to the printer unless specified to the contrary in writing.

7. There will be charges for all alterations.

8. Proofs supplied will be submitted with the original copy. Customer must check proofs when they are ready, returning proofs to the press on time. There is usually a charge for this extra step.

9. Color must be proofed for accuracy and approved by the customer prior to the print-run.

10. Over- and under-runs will not exceed 10%, or the percent agreed upon in writing. The account will be adjusted for over- and under-runs.

11. All work will be insured unless a disclaimer is filed.

12. Shipping is through UPS. or FOB. from the printer or binder.

13. Both parties will adhere to production schedules.

14. There will be extra charges for any mistakes due to customer's improperly-prepared material.

15. Payment schedules are to be outlined in the contract. All claims must be made within 15 days.

16. The printer's liability is limited to the cost of the job. No liability for lost contracts with distributors or bookstores, or lost revenue resulting from these, is the printer's. A lien will be placed on all orders not paid for.

17. The printer accepts no responsibility for copyright infringements.

Getting Quotes

Every wise consumer comparison shops. It's no different when looking for the best book-printing deal.

Presses are happy to provide you with quotes for your project free of charge—as long as you don't make a pest of yourself. If you request quotes by mail, use a business letterhead with your publisher SAN and ISBN (see details in Part 11—Headache in a Can: Marketing). Presses will fall all over themselves to please you. Don't be surprised if you get phone calls from them in addition to printed quotations.

You may be quite shocked with the range of quotations. Prices can vary by as much as 600%—all the more reason to shop around. One press may quote $450.00 for a 200-book print-run of 64-page 5$^{1}/_{2}$" x 8$^{1}/_{2}$" books; another may want $2,000.00. That's quite a range.

But, keep in mind that the least expensive printing press isn't always the way to go. Most presses will provide a free sample copy of a book of similar dimensions and page-count as the one you want quotes for. Look at the book. If you get goose bumps thinking of your book looking just like the sample copy—and the prices are reasonable—consider this press over one that does a so-so job for less. Remember, appearance is your first selling tool; it's all you have until someone actually reads your book and publicly raves about it.

Many presses will not do print-runs under 500 copies. Others will go as low as 200 or 150 copies; a handful even do 50 copies. You will have to take this into consideration when requesting quotes. Since you won't know the press minimum before you write, ask for quotes for 100, 200, 500, and 1,000 copies. You'll hit a nerve somewhere.

Know the specs of your book: page count, paper type, dimensions (untrimmed), kind of cover, cover colors, cover coating, artwork to be screened, and type of binding. You will not only have to put the specs in writing, but you may get a phone call from the press. You may photocopy the form on the next page for your use. Getting information on the press is especially critical to setting up your book. Request quotes and decide which press you will use *before* laying-out your book.

Print Quality Variations Table

	BASIC	GOOD	PREMIUM	SHOWCASE
	EVERYDAY FLYERS, COPIES	MAGAZINES, BOOKS PHOTOS DECENT	SLICK MAGAZINES VERY SHARP PHOTOS	COFFEE TABLE BOOKS PHOTOS MATCH ORIGINALS
Register—4 color	± 1/16"	± 1/100"	none	none
Register— Crossovers, backups	± 1/8"	± 1/16"	± 1/32"	none
Ink Density	some	slight	precise	precise
Ink Density— Across Sheet	some—up to 25%	slight—up to 5%	uniform—100%	uniform—100%
Ink Density— Throughout Print-run	some	slight	none	none
Large Solids, Tints, Halftones	thin, uneven mottling, ghosting	occasional mottling, ghosts	none	none
Flaws	scumming, setoff, other flaws	hickies, rare flaws	rare hickey, no other	rare hickey, no other
Photo Halftones	reduced contrast, detail, and sharpness	good contrast, sharpness, shadow detail	very sharp, excellent contrast, shadow detail	match originals
Photos—4 Color	—	slightly reduced contrast, detail	excellent sharpness, contrast, detail	excellent sharpness, contrast, detail
Folding Accuracy	± 1/8"	± 1/16"	± 1/32"	± 1/64"
Folding Alignment	inconsistent	occasionally crooked	rarely crooked	never crooked
Trimming	± 1/16"	± 1/32"	± 1/64"	± 1/64"

Lily Splane

Request for Printing Quote

Date: _____

Business: _____

Phone: _____

Department: _____

Contact Person: _____

Title: _____

Address: _____

City: _____ State: _____ Zip: _____

FAX: _____

Give Quote as: ☐ estimate ☐ in writing ☐ firm

This is a: ☐ new job ☐ reprint ☐ revised reprint

Format supplied: ☐ manuscript ☐ camera-ready ☐ disk, program: _____

Quantity: _____

Quality: ☐ basic ☐ good ☐ premium ☐ showcase

Pages: _____ ☐ including cover ☐ plus cover ☐ self-cover

Colors: _____ Cover colors: ☐ 1 ☐ 2 ☐ 3 ☐ 4

Art: ☐ halftones ☐ line art ☐ separations ☐ photos ☐ transparencies

Special: ☐ bleeds ☐ knockouts ☐ crossovers

Required Proofs: ☐ galleys ☐ pages ☐ bluelines ☐ composite

Paper: weight: _____ color: _____ finish: _____

grade: _____ brand name: _____

Cover: weight: _____ ☐ C1S ☐ C2S

Finish: ☐ varnish ☐ laminate ☐ matte coating ☐ UV ☐ IR

Binding: ☐ none ☐ saddle-stitch ☐ spiral ☐ 3-hole punch

☐ side-stitch ☐ perfect ☐ comb ☐ paste-bind ☐ case & jacket

Tip ins: ☐ yes ☐ no

Shipping: ☐ pick up Deliver: ☐ UPS ☐ USPS ☐ FOB

Information on Press

Routine Quality: ☐ basic ☐ good ☐ premium ☐ showcase

Highest Quality Possible: ☐ basic ☐ good ☐ premium ☐ showcase

Kind of Press: ☐ Sheetfed press ☐ Web press

Sheet/roll size: _____

Number of Colors per Pass: _____

Minimum Gripper Margin: _____

Registration Tolerance: _____

Signature Imposition: _____

Color-Match System: _____

Printers Marks: ☐ inside margins ☐ outside margins

Place Business Label or Stamp Here:

File Conversions

Translating files across computer platforms is no longer a problem. Most modern program files are transparent across computer platforms; there is no need to convert them. The only thing to watch for is embedded ASCII codes that don't translate properly from Wintel machines to Macintosh or vice versa.

If you are submitting a manuscript to someone else for typesetting and layout (some printing presses offer this service), file conversion might be necessary. Most high-end word processors (Microsoft Word® and Corel WordPerfect®) will read files from most other word processors.

On the other hand, page-layout programs are not so agreeable. InDesign® files have to stay in InDesign; at this printing, no other program could read Adobe InDesign files. InDesign can open Pagemaker 7 files directly, converting them on-the-fly. If you absolutely *must* transfer one page-layout file to another page-layout program, you can *export* the entire text—preserving all typesetting and formatting—as RTF (rich text format). Then, you can import the RTF file into the other program. You will, however, lose your layout and any placed or inline graphics.

PostScript Files

If you are planning to have your book output on a Linotronic Imagesetter, you may want to print your book to a PostScript file, rather than to your laser or inkjet printer. PostScript files that can be read by almost any high-end Imagesetter. That's the good news.

The bad news is that PostScript files are nearly *seven times* the size of InDesign files. That means that the 3-MB chapter that fits on a jump drive will be 21 MB as a PostScript file. With the addition of all your graphics, your CD or jump drive will fill up fast.

The biggest trend in publishing these days is Portable Document Format. Adobe Acrobat Reader, available for either Windows or Mac at no charge from Adobe's web-site (WWW.ADOBE.COM) will allow anyone on any computer with any installed fonts, to view these files. Your beautifully designed book in PDF format will look *identical* to the original in layout format, with all fonts and graphics faithfully displayed. Saved for printout, PDF files are becoming a more common way for publishers to archive, transfer, and publish their books.

With Adobe Acrobat full version, you can write and edit PDF files and distribute your books to anyone in the world—it's even possible to lock your files with a password so only authorized users can print your files, or you can disable copy and pasting snippets of text to another application.

Quality Copy Services

Staples	Office Depot
1-800-333-3330	1-800-685-8800
WWW.STAPLES.COM	WWW.OFFICEDEPOT.COM

Small Printing Presses

Æ Press
995-H Detroit Avenue
Concord, CA 94518

American Literary Press
11419 Cronridge Drive, #10
Owings Mills, MD 21117

Bayport Press, Inc.
645-D Marsat Court
Chula Vista, CA 91911-4649

Camelot Book Factory
39-B Coolidge Avenue
Ormond Beach, FL 32174

The Country Press, Inc.
P.O. Box 489
Middleboro, MA 02346

Evanston Publishing, Inc.
1216 Hinman Avenue
Evanston, IL 60202

International Printers
10225 Greenleaf
Santa Fe Springs, CA 90670-1208

National Writer's Network
Sandra Whelchel
1450 South Havana, Suite 620
Aurora, CO 80012

Network Printers
205 West Highland Avenue
Milwaukee, WI 53203

North American Book
   Manufacturing, Inc.
24–30 Brooklyn Queens
Expressway West
Woodside, NY 11377

Premier Printing Corporation
Dana C. Cordrey
P.O. Box 9726
370 Clifford Park
Brea, CA 92622

Professional Press
P.O. Box 4371
Chapel Hill, NC 27515-4371

Quintessence Publishing
Irene Bilke
356 Bunker Hill Mine Road
Amador City, CA 95601

Writers Publishing Service
Thomas Aaron
1512 Western Avenue
P.O Box 1273
Seattle, WA 98111

This is far from an exhaustive list of printing presses. For a more comprehensive listing, search online or look in the reference section of your library for a current copy of *The Literary Marketplace (LMP)*.

Print-On-Demand (POD)

By far the newest and least costly method of printing books is print-on-demand (POD). You're going to hate me for this, but with POD production, you can forget about everything you have thus-far learned about color separations, paper, and printing presses. POD employs digital files (usually PDFs), usually uploaded to the business website. You'll have far fewer decisions to make, because there are far fewer choices as to trim-size, paper type, and other details. Print-on-demand is a boon to the first-time self-publisher. It is not, however, a suitable method for printing truly professional-looking books to market to libraries, some universities, or some high-end retail outlets. And if you really do have your heart set on making a gorgeous coffee-table picture/art book, look elsewhere—POD just isn't up to it. Case-bound binding is rarely available, so paperback and saddle-stitched are usually the only available bindings. In addition, POD-produced books are ineligible for Cataloging-in-Publication with the Library of Congress. More on the POD option in "Part 12—Electronic Publishing."

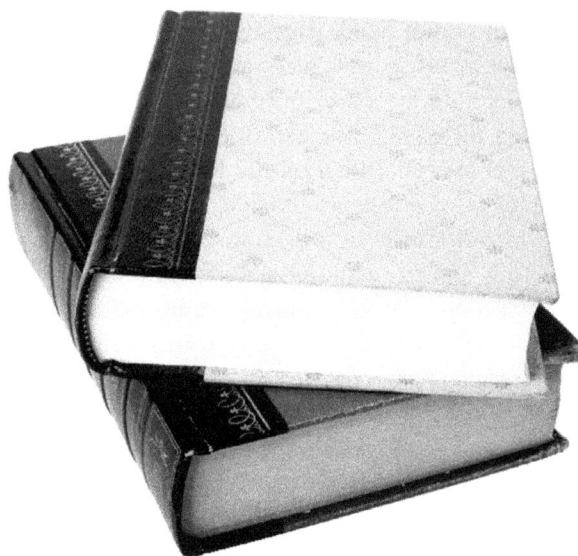

Part 10

Book Binding

Your Bound and Finished Book

Binding Methods

A book is only a collection of galleys until it is somehow bound. There are several binding formats. The majority of bookstores and book distributors will accept only perfect- and case-bound books; other bindings either do not hold up well, are hard to ship, warehouse, and shelve, or simply look too cheap and unprofessional.

- Saddle Stitch ....staples through the center fold, as in a pamphlet
- Side Stitch ....pages stapled at left edge
- Loose Leaf ....pages punched for a three-ring binder
- Spiral......................wire or plastic
- Comb (GBC).........plastic
- Paste Bind ....booklets glued at folds
- Perfect....................standard notched and glued softcover (paperback)
- Burst Perfect..........paperback; signatures not trimmed at left edge
- Case........................standard hard cover with binder's board, with jacket

Hokey Binding Methods

Saddle-stitched, paste-bound, and loose-leaf booklets and books sell best to unsuspecting mail order customers. Book distributors and bookstores will not take them. The exception is loose-leaf cookbooks and instruction manuals. Sometimes short informational booklets are accepted by local specialty stores, such as health food stores, auto parts stores, or garden supply shops. But, unless you have a market, forget about these binding methods.

Comb Binding

Comb binding has not gained much acceptance with book distributors or bookstores. The plastic combs tend to tangle in shipping. Unless the title is silk-screen printed on the spine, shelving comb-bound books spine-out in bookstores makes them invisible and difficult to sell. (Bookstores are reluctant to shelve books cover out—it takes up too much shelf space.) The pages of comb-bound books also tend to loosen from the binding through handling by browsers. Comb-bound books are suited best to direct mail order.

Comb Size	Sheet Capacity	Book Pages
$1/4$"	20	40
$5/16$"	40	80
$3/8$"	55	110
$1/2$"	90	180
$5/8$"	120	240
1"	200	400

Perfect Binding

The binding method that affords the most durability plus cost-effectiveness is perfect-binding. Perfect-binding consists of gluing a C1S cover onto a stack of glued signatures. Most independent publishers, as well as distributors and bookstores, prefer this kind of binding: It is inexpensive, so the cover price can be kept reasonable, and it is fairly durable. Designing covers for perfect-bound books is an artistic and frequently pleasurable experience.

Case-Binding

Hardcover books are case-bound: Signatures are glued together and either glued or stitched into a cloth- or plastic-covered binder's board. Case-binding is very durable—libraries love them—but is frequently cost-prohibitive for the independent publisher. Colorful paper jackets often cover the case-binding, further escalating costs. Cover prices for hard-bound self-published books are so high, few sell.

Aggravation in a Nutshell: Signatures

Imposition

Books may be typeset and layed-out one page after another, but the pages have to later be set up in *signatures* so that many pages can be printed on a huge sheet and folded at the press. The signature pattern (4-up, 8-up, 16-up) is called the *imposition*. Grouping pages in a signature is called *stripping*.

Proper imposition is required for offset printing, and if photocopying booklets. If pages are 8½" by 11", then *do not* impose them for the printer. Also do not send pages printed or glued back-to-back, to an offset press. The pressman will not be impressed or amused.

Folded signatures are in booklets and pamphlets; folded and *gathered* signatures (sometimes referred to as F & Gs) compose a book; *inserted* signatures make up a catalog.

Folded signatures are trimmed on three or four sides, depending on the bindery.

The most common signature size is 8-up. This means that eight pages are on the front, and eight pages are on the back of a single big sheet that runs through the press. The plates are made 8-up also, so only one pass per side is required.

Most word processors cannot set up files in signatures; page-layout programs can. If you are making your book in a word processor, you will have to cut the pages and glue them to a standard-sized sheet in the proper signature order. Use rubber cement or another glue that won't wrinkle the paper.

Signature Page Folds

Signature Folds

# PAGES	1ST FOLD	2ND FOLD	3RD FOLD
4-up (8)	Down	Over, Left–Right	none
8-up (16)	Over, L–R	Down	Over, L–R

FRONT of Parent Sheet—4-up Signature

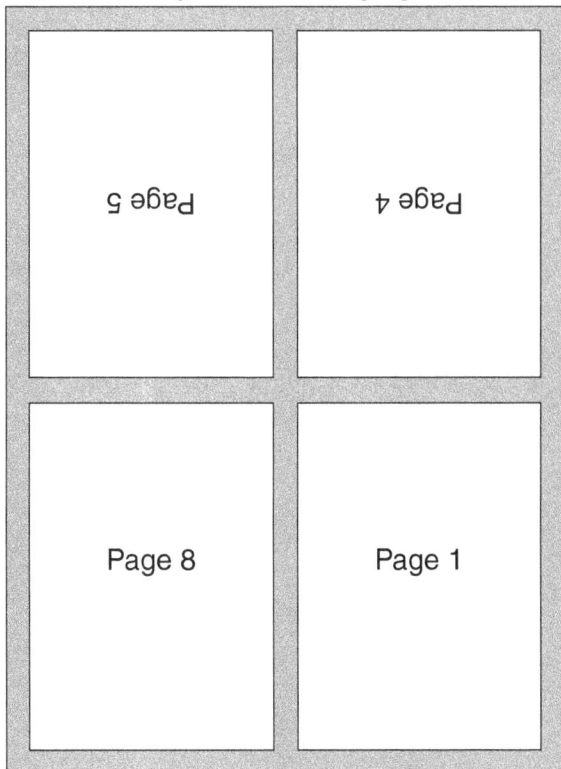

Page 5   Page 4

Page 8   Page 1

BACK of Parent Sheet—4-up Signature

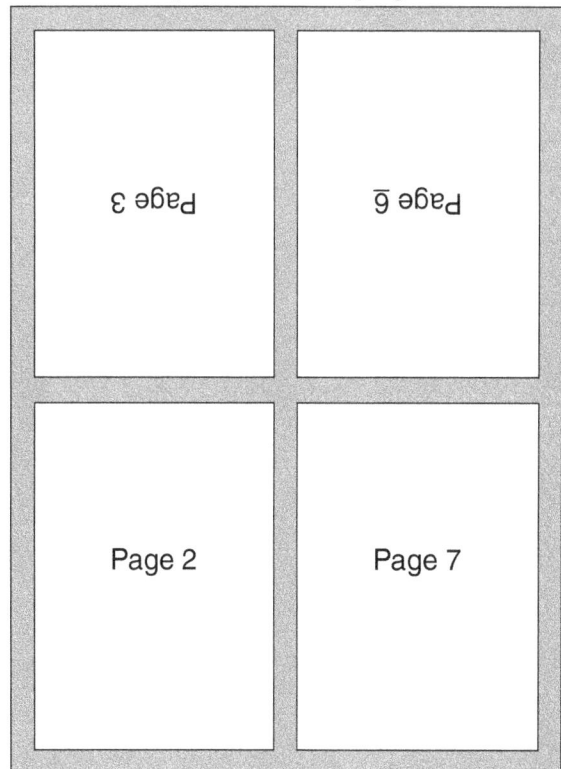

Page 3   Page 6

Page 2   Page 7

Lily Splane

Page 5	Page 12	Page 9	Page 8
Page 4	Page 13	Page 16	Page 1

Above: FRONT *of 8-up Signature Parent Sheet.* **Below:** BACK *of 8-up Signature Parent Sheet*

Page 7	Page 10	Page 11	Page 6
Page 2	Page 15	Page 14	Page 3

Saddle-Stitched Catalog
Single Signature—2-up

12 half-pages, back-to-back on 8½" by 11" sheets—Photocopy or Sheet-fed Offset
for a 12-page 5½" by 8½" booklet

| | FRONT | | BACK | | | |
SIGNATURE	RECTO	VERSO	VERSO	RECTO	SPREAD	PRESS SHEETS
one	1	12	2	11	1, 2	1, 2
two	3	10	4	9	3, 4	3, 4
three	5	8	6	7	5, 6	5, 6

Saddle-Stitched Catalog
Single Signature—2-up

32 half-pages back-to-back on 8½" by 11" sheets—Photocopy or Sheet-fed Offset
for a 32-page 5½" by 8½" booklet

| | FRONT | | BACK | | | |
SIGNATURE	RECTO	VERSO	VERSO	RECTO	SPREAD	PRESS SHEETS
one	1	32	2	31	1, 2	1, 2
two	3	30	4	29	3, 4	3, 4
three	5	28	6	27	5, 6	5, 6
four	7	26	8	25	7, 8	7, 8
five	9	24	10	23	9, 10	9, 10
six	11	22	12	21	11, 12	11, 12
seven	13	20	14	19	13, 14	13, 14
eight	15	18	12	17	15, 16	15, 16

Eight-Page Signature Setup—4-up

8 half-pages, printed back-to-back on 11" by 17" sheets—Photocopy or Sheet-fed Offset for a 112-page 5½" by 8½" book

SIGNATURE	FRONT		BACK		SPREADS	PRESS SHEET
	VERSO	RECTO	VERSO	RECTO		
one	8	1	2	7	1	1
	6	3	4	5	2	
two	16	9	10	15	3	2
	14	11	12	13	4	
three	24	17	18	23	5	3
	22	19	20	21	6	
four	32	25	26	31	7	4
	30	27	28	29	8	
five	40	33	34	39	9	5
	38	35	36	37	10	
six	48	41	42	47	11	6
	46	43	44	45	12	
seven	56	49	50	55	13	7
	54	51	52	53	14	
eight	64	57	58	63	15	8
	62	59	60	61	16	
nine	72	65	66	71	17	9
	70	67	68	69	18	
ten	80	73	74	79	19	10
	78	75	76	77	20	
eleven	88	81	82	87	21	11
	86	83	84	85	22	
twelve	96	89	90	95	23	12
	94	91	92	93	24	
thirteen	104	97	98	103	25	13
	102	99	100	101	26	
fourteen	112	105	106	111	27	14
	110	107	108	109	28	

Sixteen-Page Signature Setup—8-up

16 half-pages, back-to-back on 22" by 35" sheets*—Sheet-fed Offset
for a 112-page 5½" by 8½" book

| | FRONT | | BACK | | | |
SIGNATURE	VERSO	RECTO	VERSO	RECTO	SPREADS	PRESS SHEETS
one	16	1	2	15	1, 2	1
	14	3	4	13	3, 4	
	12	5	6	11	5, 6	
	10	7	8	9	7, 8	
two	32	17	18	31	9, 10	2
	30	19	20	29	11, 12	
	28	21	22	27	13, 14	
	26	23	24	25	15, 16	
three	48	33	34	47	17, 18	3
	46	35	36	45	19, 20	
	44	37	38	43	21, 22	
	42	39	40	41	23, 24	
four	64	49	50	63	25, 26	4
	62	51	52	61	27, 28	
	60	53	54	59	29, 30	
	58	55	56	57	31, 32	
five	80	65	66	79	33, 34	5
	78	67	68	77	35, 36	
	76	69	70	75	37, 38	
	74	71	72	73	39, 40	
six	96	81	82	95	41, 42	6
	94	83	84	93	43, 44	
	92	85	86	91	45, 46	
	90	87	88	89	47, 48	
seven	112	97	98	111	49, 50	7
	110	99	100	109	51, 52	
	108	101	102	107	53, 54	
	106	103	104	105	55, 56	

* Actual sheet size is 25" by 38" and requires trimming.

Thirty-Two-Page Signature Setup—16-up

32 half-pages, back-to-back on 44" by 70" sheets (after cutting)—Web Offset
for a 128-page 5½" by 8½" book

SIGNATURE	OUTSIDE		INSIDE		SPREADS	PRESS SHEETS
	VERSO	RECTO	VERSO	RECTO		
one	32	1	2	31	1, 2	1
	30	3	4	29	3, 4	
	28	5	6	27	5, 6	
	26	7	8	25	7, 8	
	24	9	10	23	9, 10	
	22	11	12	21	11, 12	
	20	13	14	19	13, 14	
	18	15	16	17	15, 16	
two	64	33	34	63	17, 18	2
	62	35	36	61	19, 20	
	60	37	38	59	21, 22	
	58	39	40	57	23, 24	
	56	41	42	55	25, 26	
	54	43	44	53	27, 28	
	52	45	46	51	29, 30	
	50	47	48	49	31, 32	
three	96	65	66	95	33, 34	3
	94	67	68	93	35, 36	
	92	69	70	91	37, 38	
	90	71	72	89	39, 40	
	88	73	74	87	41, 42	
	86	75	76	85	43, 44	
	84	77	78	83	45, 46	
	82	79	80	81	47, 48	
four	128	97	98	127	49, 50	4
	126	99	100	125	51, 52	
	124	101	102	123	53, 54	
	122	103	104	121	55, 56	
	120	105	106	119	57, 58	
	118	107	108	117	59, 60	
	116	109	110	115	61, 62	
	114	111	112	113	63, 64	

Trim

Folded signatures are trimmed on a *cutting board*. A *lift* of folded signatures (up to 3" thick) is held fast under pressure and the edges trimmed to specifications—commonly $\frac{1}{16}$"–$\frac{1}{8}$" on each of four sides, for a total of $\frac{1}{8}$"–$\frac{1}{4}$" vertically, and $\frac{1}{8}$"–$\frac{1}{4}$" horizontally. This means that your $5\frac{1}{2}$" by $8\frac{1}{2}$" book will actually be $5\frac{3}{8}$" by $8\frac{3}{8}$" to $5\frac{1}{4}$" by $8\frac{1}{4}$", depending on press tolerances. Refer to the "Print Quality Variations Table" in "Part 9—The Printing Press," for details on what to expect with trim size at the kind of press you plan to use.

The amount of trim varies with the press; take this into account when preparing page margins.

The amount of trimming is especially important to know before designing book covers. Miscalculations or misinformation can result in off-centered cover art that looks sloppy and amateurish.

Scoring and Tipping In

Paper over 0.005" (such as coverstock) may be *scored* so it will fold and bend easily. You will be charged a nominal fee for scoring.

In magazines and some paperback books, gluing sheets to a page in a signature is known as *tipping in*. Reply cards and reader surveys are examples.

Creep

Booklets over 12 sheets (48 pages) are subject to a phenomenon known as *creep*. Creep is the subtle weaseling of folded sheets from the middle towards the outside edge. Actually, any number of inserted pages is subject to some degree of creep. The fatter the booklet, the greater the creep. If you haven't set your outside margins deep enough, after trimming, the outside margins of the center-most pages can be nearly flush with the text.

In burst-perfect binding, the signatures are not trimmed at the inner fold. These signatures are subject to only slight creep.

Varnishing, UV or IR Coating, and Laminating

Books should be varnished or covered in something shiny and slippery that makes them attractive and durable. Slick covers are also less prone to scuffing in shipping.

Cover varnishing is a wash applied at the press. It is the least expensive of cover coatings—frequently under a dime a book.

UV (ultraviolet) and IR (infrared) coating, as well as plastic laminating, is done at the bindery. These cover coatings impart a lustrous finish to the cover and are very durable. UV coating is less expensive than plastic laminating, but both will drive up the production cost and cover price of your books.

Rules for Writers

Just for Fun

- Remember to never split an infinitive.
- The passive voice should never be used.
- Do not put statements in the negative form.
- Verbs have to agree with their subject.
- Proofread carefully to see if you words out.
- If you reread your work, you can find on rereading a great deal of repetition can be avoided by rereading and editing.
- A writer must not shift your point of view.
- And don't start a sentence with a conjunction.
- Remember, too, a preposition is a terrible word to end a sentence with.
- Don't overuse exclamation marks!!
- Place pronouns as close as possible, especially in long sentences, of 10 or more words, to their antecedents.
- Writing carefully, dangling participles must be avoided.
- If any word is improper at the end of a sentence, a linking verb is.
- Take the bull by the hand and avoid mixing metaphors.
- Avoid trendy locutions that sound flaky.
- Everyone should be careful to use a singular pronoun with singular nouns in their writing.
- Always pick on the correct idiom.
- The adverb always follows the verb.
- Last but not least, avoid clichés like the plague, even if your life depends on it.
- Never use a preposition to end a sentence with.
- Avoid annoying alliteration.
- Don't verb nouns.
- Don't use no double negatives.
- Make each pronoun agree with their antecedent.
- When dangling, watch your participles.
- Don't use commas, which aren't necessary.
- Verbs has to agree with their subjects.
- About those sentence fragments.
- Try to not ever split infinitives.
- Its important to use apostrophe's correctly.
- Always read what you have written to see if you've any words out.
- Correct spelling is esential.
- Proofread you writing.
- Between you and i, case is important.
- Verbs has to agree with their antecedents.

Part 11

Headache in a Can: Marketing & Management

This Little Publisher Went to Market...

Distribution

Nothing strikes terror in the hearts of self-publishers like the question, "Hey, how you gonna sell this thing?"

You've written, typeset, layed-out, and printed your book. Your book is smooth and beautiful in your hands—its cousins sit coolly in boxes in a corner of your living room—and you're feeling pretty triumphant about the whole experience.

That was the easy part. Now you need *buyers*.

Book Distributors

Book distributors consign with publishers to distribute their books. There is no up-front charge for this service; distributors get a percentage of the cover price of your book only for the copies sold. This percentage averages 15% *plus* the 40% discount distributors in turn offer bookstores. That means that you will be selling your books to distributors at a 55% discount off the cover price, leaving you a paltry 45%—from which you must deduct production costs before figuring profit. (See the "Pricing Strategies and Profit Calculation" section later in this chapter.)

In addition to this big bite, you must pay for all shipping to the distributor. Fortunately, distributors then pay the shipping to bookstores and other book outlets across the country.

At first glance, it doesn't seem cost-effective to involve distributors. But, consider how many markets distributors can reach. The average number of markets per distributor is roughly 5,000. (The giants, Baker & Taylor and Ingram, cover thousands more the world over.) If only one copy of your book sells to each of them, you've sold 5,000 copies—in a couple of months, with minimal capital outlay for mailings or advertising.

Obviously, not all book outlets will want books on every subject. Distributors can target your market for you, ensuring that auto parts stores as well as book stores know about your car repair book. Distributors usually release catalogs and do reviews on books they carry, much to the publisher's benefit. In addition to annual catalogs and monthly forthcoming title reports, some distributors have special catalogs dedicated to a specific topic, such as New Age titles, that zero in on appropriate buyers.

Most distributors do not ask for exclusive rights to market your books, but a few do. Independent Publishers Group is one of these. Carefully consider the consequences of exclusive distributorship before signing the contract.

Distributors do the hard work: finding customers and shipping to them. You will only have to deal with two to eight distributors. The reduction in paperwork alone is worth a measly 15% off the top.

Distributors demand good quality, well-written books. They prefer perfect-bound books, as other bindings fall apart and case-bound books from self-publishers must be priced too high to recover production costs.

Distributors will pay you 45% of the cover price for every book they sell—*not* all the books you ship to them (unless all are sold). Payment for books is 30–90 days after the end of the month in which they are sold. You will have to bill the distributor, as they rarely cough up payment spontaneously, even though you have enclosed an invoice with the shipment.

The time lag between production and payment is sometimes a hardship for self-publishers. For this reason, set up accounts with a few distributors, and stagger them so you'll have enough money coming in every month to print more books. Otherwise, you'll find yourself out of stock waiting for money to drift in one check at a time, unable to print more books until you've saved enough for the next print-run. Not a good situation. Both you and the distributor are "doing books" to make money. Distributors don't like being told that "there has been an unforeseen delay in the production schedule." They may cancel your contract if you delay too many times.

To get distributors interested, send a well-designed flyer describing your book, including a summary of the contents, size, page count, binding, cover price, and ISBN. Offer to send a free sample copy, and include a postpaid postcard for them to use to get it. Write a short blurb about your book on your letterhead and beat the bushes for distribution contracts.

The following distributor list is far from complete. A complete listing of distributors may be found online or in the *LMP (Literary Marketplace).*

Baker and Taylor—
Eastern Division
6 Kirby Avenue
Somerville, NJ 08872

Baker and Taylor—
Western Division
380 Edison Way
Reno, NV 89564

Book Dynamics, Inc.
Mr. Robert Crews
330 Dalziel Road
Linden, NJ 07036

Book Passage
51 Tamal Vista Blvd.
Corte Madera, CA 94925

Book Travelers West
Mr. C. Thomas Fritzinger
9551 Landfall Drive
Huntington Beach, CA 92646

Bookazine Book Distributors
303 West 10th Street
New York, NY 10014

BookPeople
7900 Edgewater Drive
Oakland, CA 94621

Bookslinger
2402 University, #507
St. Paul, MN 55114

Devorss & Company
P.O. Box 550
Marina Del Rey, CA 90294

Distributors
The Talman Company, Inc.
131 Spring Street, Suite 20E-N
New York, NY 10012

Gordon Soules
Book Publishers Ltd.
1352-B Marine Drive
West Vancouver, BC
Canada V7T 1B5

Independent Publishers Group
Mr. Mark S. Suchomel
814 Franklin Street
Chicago, IL 60610

Independent Publishers Mkg.
Ms. Donna Montgomery
6824 Oakland Avenue
Edina, MN 55435

Ingram Book Company
1125 Heil Quaker Road
La Vergne, TN 37086

Inland Book Company
Mr. David Wilk
Box 120261
East Haven, CT 06512

Island Pacific NW
P.O. Box 999
Eastsound, WA 98245

Moving Books
P.O. Box 20037
948 S. Doris Street
Seattle, WA 98108

National Association of
Independent Publishers' Reps.
Mr. Ralph Woodward
Box 2436
Framingham, MA 01701

National Book Network, Inc.
Mr. Jed Lyons
4720 Boston Way, # A
Lanham, MD 20706-4310

New Leaf Distributing Co.
5425 Tulane Drive SW
Atlanta, GA 30336

Pacific Crest Distributors
P.O. Box 380
Redmond, WA 98073

Pacific Pipeline
8030 South 228th Street
Kent, WA 98032

Practical Books
Mr. Michael Woodhouse
361 Orrong Road
Kewdale, WA
Australia 6105

Publishers Distribution Service
Mr. Jerrold Jenkins
121 East Front Street, Ste 202
Traverse City, MI 49684

Pyramid Distributors
1577 Barry Avenue
Los Angeles, CA 90025

Quality Books, Inc.
918 Sherwood Drive
Lake Bluff, IL 60044

Seven Hills Distributors
49 Central Avenue
Cincinnati, OH 45202

Small Press Distribution Co.
Ms. Lisa Domitrovich
1814 San Pablo Avenue
Berkeley, CA 94702

Sunbelt Publications
P.O. Box 191126
San Diego, CA 92119

The Booklegger
13100 Grass Valley Ave.
Grass Valley, CA 95945

The Distributors
702 South Michigan
South Bend, IN 46601

WHSMITH
York House
113 Merton Street
Toronto, Ontario
Canada M4S 1A8

Colleges

College bookstores stock not only textbooks for instruction, but supplementary texts and general-audience books.

If you are qualified to teach and have written a textbook or manual that may interest other instructors, solicit the instructors of the particular department of your subject, as well as the college bookstores. If instructors show an interest in using the book, the bookstore will be encouraged to stock it—otherwise, if they show no interest in your textbook or manual, seek elsewhere. There is no need for college bookstores to stock textbooks or manuals that instructors won't use in classes.

Other kinds of books may be of interest to college bookstores; write to them or visit the bookstore manager.

College textbooks sell for a 20% discount to college bookstores if you are one of the Big Guys; they sell for a 40% discount if you're an independent publisher. Payment terms are usually net 30–45 days, but can be longer.

Your library has references listing colleges throughout the United States. You may purchase an excellent book titled, *20014–2015 Accredited Institutions of Post-Secondary Education: Programs, Candidates,* published by the American Council on Education. This book lists all public and private junior colleges and universities in the United States, as well as a few foreign schools. This reference book is available through:

Oryx Press
4041 North Central Avenue
Phoenix, AZ 85012-3397
(800) 279-6799
(602) 265-2651

Libraries

Libraries are always eager for durable, well-written and popular general-audience, children's, and technical books. Libraries will buy several copies, perhaps dozens for an entire region or county. They usually get a 20–25% discount and pay in 30–45 days.

Quality Books, a distributor listed on the previous page, sells to libraries exclusively.

Your best bet for finding library addresses is to compile a mailing list from the authority on publishing, the *Literary Market Place*. Bowker also publishes the *American Library Directory*. Both volumes are available in the reference section of your library.

Bookstores

If you feel energetic enough, you may want to sell directly to bookstores in your neighborhood. Independent neighborhood bookstores are frequently happy to carry a local author's books. A 40% discount is industry-standard for bookstores. This discount allows for returns if the books are not sold within a specified period (see "Returns" section). A 50% discount may be extended with the stipulation that no returns are allowed.

Give the bookstore manager a poster or a flyer to paste in the window or hang somewhere to attract attention to your book. Mention on the poster that you are a local writer.

Large chain bookstores such as Cole's, Dalton, and Waldenbooks have been reluctant in past years to stock self-published books. Shelf space is a valuable asset and is usually reserved for big sellers by authors such as Danielle Steele and Stephen King. This is how the big bookstore chains make their money—an unknown author can't possibly bring in enough revenue to even pay for his or her book's shelf space.

Or so it was arrogantly believed...until the *Roadkill Cookbook* came on the scene. Bookstores can't seem to keep this self-published, comb-bound laughfest stocked. It's sold out as soon as it's on the shelf. There's a lesson here—for both bookstores and publishers.

Some chain bookstores will deal with independent publishers if the books are high-quality and well written on subjects that are in demand. The chains, however, would prefer to deal with distributors rather than with you.

Direct Mail

Stories of direct-mail publishing millionaires abound. Don't you believe them. For every self-publisher who has scored big-time with his or her books through direct mail, there are at least a hundred who failed miserably.

Direct-mail selling is grueling. Statistically, you may expect about a 1–2% response from each advertisement mailing. This means that for every 100 flyers you mail out, one or two people will order your book. The cost of printing and mailing brochures quickly puts you in the hole. Unless you are financially comfortable, very patient, and have an up-to-date and tightly-targeted mailing list, direct mail will break you. It isn't recommended for beginners.

A cousin of direct mail is selling through classified or display ads in specialty magazines. The success rate of this strategy is variable. Everything depends on properly targeting your ad campaign and writing irresistible ad copy. Marketing experts have also determined that consumers need to see an ad *seven consecutive times* before they will respond by ordering the advertised product.

You must take great care selecting in which magazines to place your ad. A book on astrology to reduce stress would not sell from an ad placed in psychology or therapy magazines—it will be taken seriously in a New Age magazine or an astrology magazine. A nutrition book sells better from health and nutrition magazines than from science or medical magazines. However, you may also need to consider your audience's interests. Would a busy mother buy a quilting book from an ad in a hobbies and crafts magazine? Maybe. Quilting is a hobby. But she might also buy it from an ad in a child care magazine, a women's magazine, a sewing magazine, a homemaker's magazine, or even a homesteader's back-to-nature magazine.

Specialty Shops

Specialty shops usually carry books on their own specialty. No big revelation there. Health food stores carry nutrition books, auto parts stores carry repair manuals and even coffee table books on classic cars. Pharmacies carry books and booklets on illness and even vitamins and nutrition matters. Would the local nursery like your southern California garden pest book?

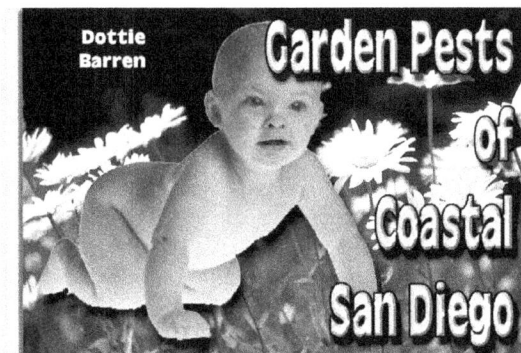

Catalogs

Gift catalogs from all over the country carry books. Surprisingly, most of these books are off-the-wall independently-published books that sell for a reasonable price and attract impulse buyers. *Joel's Journal and Fart Book*, *Fart Proudly*, *The Dirty Song Book*, *The Anarchist's Cookbook*, and *The Art of Getting Even* are examples of the wacky titles you may find in gift catalogs.

Specialty catalogs also carry books much as specialty shops do. Look into a few catalog mail-order companies that might want to carry your book.

Premiums

Though often regarded as a last resort, offering books as premiums for some other purchase can be a way to unload an overstock. It can also be a sneaky way of exposing your book to lots of people.

Premium discounts are steep. Retailers will generally give you 25% (that's a 75% discount) of your cover price and demand hundreds or thousands of copies all at once. If you can afford to do this (printing is much cheaper in 5,000–10,000-book print-runs—each 64-page 5½" x 8½" book can cost as little as 59¢), you can move thousands of copies fairly quickly and clean up in a hurry.

Needless to say, such a strategy can be exhausting. You will spend thousands of dollars and many hours packing and shipping cartons of books in a one-shot deal.

The one good thing about this kind of selling is the sales record. Should you ever want to approach another publisher to take over your book, the sheer volume of sales will be impressive. Enough volume can translate into a dazzling cash flow as well.

More complete sources on book marketing:

Book Publishing Resource Guide by John Kremer Ad-Lib Publications 51 N. Fifth Street Fairfield, IA 52556-3226 1-800-669-0773	*Success Strategies* *to Increase Your Sales* (6-hour audio & workbook) Tom and Marilyn Ross Communication Creativity P.O. Box 909 Buena Vista, CO 81211

Free Publicity

Never underestimate the power of free publicity. The media is available and waiting to print a short story on you or interview you about your book.

Radio interviews are the best and most productive publicity you can get. People who listen to radio listen to learn something, rather than be passively amused as televidiots do. Radio listeners buy books.

Your local newspaper may want to do a story on you...that you can talk the reporter into putting over the newswire, and *poof!* you're suddenly syndicated in the national news. (The reporter wants his or her byline out there as much as you want the story out there.)

Cable TV Community Access channels frequently interview authors and other artists. These shows are televised several times a week and your interview may repeat dozens of times, sometimes for *years*.

Have you written a compelling or pertinent book that Oprah Winfrey might be intrigued enough to call you about? There are literally dozens of talk shows on television now, not to mention interview segments on local newscasts. Write to a few of these televised shows. Unknown authors can be just as entertaining as glitter people. You never know until you try....

Keep in mind that if you are interviewed on TV or radio, audiences must have a way to order your book. Provide your distributor's toll-free phone number (BookPeople's is 1-800-999-4650), or the name of the bookstores where your book is carried.

Warn bookstores and distributors in advance that you will be appearing on TV or being interviewed on the radio—they will need to order more copies of your book. If things turn out really well, a book-signing may follow.

If you have serious bucks, you may even want to hire a publicist—a hot shot who goes around tooting your horn for you until someone takes you seriously. Publicists do all the footwork and paperwork, leaving you free to write more books. Their duties include preparing an entire media kit with a press release, fact sheet, and author bio, among other documents.

There are good publicists and lousy publicists. Publicists may charge a $,1000–$,5000 per month retainer. Get references and utterly interrogate your prospective horn-tooter before parting with that kind of cash.

Or, do it yourself. Only you can be enough in love with your book to make it sound good to someone else. Press releases can do wonders, especially if you have an angle that's a bit unusual—a gimmick, if you will. Consider the press release for *Anaphase II Publishing* on the next page.

*** PRESS   RELEASE ***

Client: Anaphase II Publishing
Date: August 24, 1995
Contact: Lily Splane
           (619) 501-5885

"SMALL PRESS DEDICATED TO DISABLED COMMUNITY OPENS IN SAN DIEGO"

San Diego, CA—Owned and operated by the physically disabled, ***Anaphase II Publishing*** publishes books written by the disabled, and also provides book production and writing services (editing, rewriting, typesetting, book layout, and design.) at greatly reduced cost to low-income disabled individuals.

The small press, located in the North Park area of San Diego, will be the only book publisher in San Diego dedicated to the low-income disabled. Owned and operated by Lily Splane, a published author, ***Anaphase II*** will specialize in concise, information-intensive non-fiction books of 64–350 pages, written by disabled persons in the recognition that disability does not preclude intelligence and competence in a given field of expertise. Topics include the sciences, health, philosophy and ethics, humor, cooking, and how-to manuals.

Fiction Writer's Companion: A Concise Collection of Notes on Technique, by L.M. Shubailey, is available now. *Quantum Consciousness: A Philosophy of the Self's Potential Through Quantum Cosmology,* and *Nutritional Self-Defense: Better Health In A Stressful, Polluted, and Over-Processed World,* both written by Lily Splane, are slated for future release.

Michael Woodhouse of Practical Books in Australia, says of *Fiction Writer's Companion,* "Great book! Lots of information, tightly packed. I've just finished reading [another author's] book on fiction writing...you have taken 60 pages to say more than he did in a few hundred."

Anaphase II will be accepting manuscript submissions starting in July, 2003, with plans to publish four new titles in 2003. Manuscripts must fit the format of concise information-intensive reference or how-to manuals, and be 12,000–80,000 words on the topics of nutrition, physics, biology, cosmology, astronomy, repair/maintenance, New–Age-type philosophy with an emphasis on social ecology, and humor. Essay collections will be considered. Queries with author biographies and SASE must be submitted prior to manuscript submission.

For more information, contact Lily Splane, managing editor at
Anaphase II Publishing, 2739 Wightman Street, San Diego, CA, 92104-3526.

# # #

A press release should have a "hook line" such as you'd find in newspaper articles. The press release should be double-spaced with a space between paragraphs. Keep it as short as possible—not over 2 pages. End the report with three pound signs (###) centered at the end to let readers know there is no more and they haven't lost a page.

Send press releases to radio stations, television stations, newspapers, local magazines, national magazines, and small press magazines—literally anywhere someone might take notice. Always include a phone number. You may want to enclose a self-addressed postpaid postcard with check boxes for respondents to use requesting further information or a sample copy of your book.

Places to Send Your Press Release

Byline
Marcia Preston
Box 130596
Edmond, OK 73013

Guidelines Magazine
Susan Salaki
Box 608
Pittsburgh, MO 65724

Housewife-Writer's Forum
Deborah Haeseler
Drawer 1518
Layfayette, CA 94549

New Writer's Magazine
Sarasota Bay Publishing
George J. Hobarak
Box 5974
Sarasota, FL 34277

North American
   Bookdealer's Exchange
Bookdealer's World
Al Galasso
Box 606
Cottage Grove, OR 97424

Rising Star
Scott E. Green
47 Byledge Road
Manchester NH 03104

Scavenger's Newsletter
Janet Fox
519 Ellinwood
Osage City, KS 66523

Small Press
Meckler Corporation
Brenda Mitchell-Powell
11 Ferry Lane West
Westport, CT 06880

Small Press Review
Len Fulton
Box 100
Paradise, CA 95967

Small Publisher
Nigel Maxey
Box 1620
Pineville, WV 24874

The Editorial Eye
Ann R. Molpus
Suite 200
66 Canal Center Plaza
Alexandria, VA 22314-1578

The Writer
Sylvia K. Burack
120 Boylston Street
Boston, MA 02116

WDS Book Author's Newsletter
Writer's Digest School
Kirk Polking
1507 Dana Avenue
Cincinnati, OH 45207

West Coast Review of Books
David Dreis
Upper Terrace #6
5265 Fountain Avenue
Los Angeles, CA 90029

Writer's Info
Linda Hutton
Box 1870
Hayden, ID 83835

Writer's Journal
Minnesota Ink, Inc
Valerie Hockert
Box 9148
North St. Paul, MN 55109

Getting Books Out and Money In

Packing

OK, you're excited. You've just received your first order from a distributor. What do you do now?

If you're lucky, the distributor has ordered the exact quantity contained in one box you got from the printing press, and you never have to reopen or repack the box; you just have to relabel it and reship it. Chances are, this won't work out quite this way.

Buy boxes and good acetate or filament tape. *Buy* boxes—do *not* use old beat-up rescued-from-the-dumpster-behind-Rite-Aid-Drugs boxes. You have to look professional. *Anusol*® printed on the side of your box doesn't look professional unless you're a proctologist.

Pack books *flat*, not on their edges. Big boxes look manly and strong, so strong manly postal personnel work them over. Boxes take a lot of hell. Packing books on edge will guarantee crinkled corners and rumpled covers. Your distributor will send them back to you as unsalable.

You may want to place sheets of paper between each layer of books. This reduces scuffing and keeps the shiny new covers brilliant and colorful.

Pack books as tightly as you can without making the box bulge or the books buckle. You may have to stuff twisted ropes of paper (*not* newspaper—the ink rubs off) between the box wall and the books. The object is to keep them from shifting in the box.

Before sealing the box, put the invoice on the top of the books. The invoice should have your publisher name and address along with your SAN and ISBN, the purchase order number (your distributor or customer provides this—use it, it's very important), the name and address of the distributor or customer, the date ordered, the date you fulfilled the order (the date you closed the box, not necessarily the date you shipped it), the title of the book ordered, the book's ISBN, the quantity ordered, the quantity shipped, the full cover price, the percent discount you are giving the distributor or customer (per your agreement), the adjusted price per copy, and finally, the total for the shipment.

At the bottom of the invoice you should state the payment terms as agreed in your contract: net 30, 45, 60, or 90 days.

Seal the box with the tape (a boxing tape dispenser is invaluable) across all seams. Tape the corners and edges for strength. The box will be a bear to open, but what's inside remains unscathed.

Enter the order number on the shipping label. On the side of the box, attach a label listing the title of the book, the ISBN, the quantity enclosed, and which box this is and of how many total boxes (box 1 of 1; box 3 of 5, etc.). This last step keeps warehouse people from getting paranoid, wondering if there are more boxes in the shipment or if the one they're holding is the *only* one. (How do you keep a numbskull in suspense? I'll tell you next week.)

If you cannot ship the quantity ordered, note this on the invoice and state whether the books are permanently out of stock (OS), temporarily out of stock (TOS), or back-ordered (BO). Use these industry-standard abbreviations for the status of the shipment.

On occasion, someone may order a book with either the wrong ISBN or the wrong title. Sometimes orders come in for books years after they've gone out of print, or new editions have been released. Assume nothing. Politely inform your prospective customer of the error, send your flyers or catalog with the titles and ISBNs in plain view, and wait. If they're interested they'll reorder; if not, they probably have the wrong publisher.

Shipping

There are two ways to economically ship books—through the postal service or through UPS. UPS is faster. Fourth-class packages are presumably shipped by barge pulled by tired mules. UPS is more expensive than fourth-class Post Office book rates (almost double), but UPS takes a little more care than the Post Office. The Post Office employs enraged rhinos to stomp your boxes into confetti—but they don't charge much for the service.

Shipping rates are affected by distance. For example: From southern California, shipping a 15-pound box of books to within southern California costs less than a third the cost to New York.

U.S.P.S. 2002 Zone Chart from Zipcode 921-- (southern California)

Zip	Zone	Zip	Zone
005–098	8	703–708	7
100–212	8	710–711	6
214–268	8	712–714	7
270–324	8	716	7
325	7	717–719	6
326–342	8	720–725	7
344	8	726–731	6
346–347	8	733–738	6
349	8	739	5
350–352	7	740–741	6
354–361	7	743–768	6
362–363	8	769	5
364–372	7	770–789	6
373–374	8	790–794	5
375	7	795–796	6
376–379	8	797–812	5
380–397	7	813	4
398–399	8	814–816	5
400–402	7	820–837	5
403–418	8	838	6
420–424	7	840–844	5
425–426	8	845–847	4
427	7	850	4
430–459	8	852–853	4
460–466	7	855–857	4
467–468	8	859–860	4
469	7	863–864	3
470	8	865	4
471–472	7	870–872	5
473	8	873–874	4
474–479	7	875	5

Lily Splane

U.S.P.S. 2002 Zone Chart
from Zipcode 921-- (southern California)

Zip	Zone	Zip	Zone
480–497	8	877	5
498–507	7	878–880	4
508	6	881–885	5
509	7	889–891	3*
510–516	6	893	4*
520–528	7	894–895	4
530–532	7	897–898	4
534–535	7	900–908	2*
537–567	7	910–918	2*
570–577	6	919–921	1*
580–583	7	922–928	2*
584–588	6	930	2*
590–591	5	931–935	3*
592–595	6	936–938	3
596–598	5	939–954	4
599	6	955	5
600–620	7	956–966	4
622–639	7	967–969	8
640–642	6	970–979	5
644–649	6	980–985	6
650–653	7	986	5
654–658	6	988–989	5
660–676	6	990–992	6
677–679	5	993–994	5
680–681	6	995–998	8
683–693	6	999	7
700–701	7		

U.S.P.S. 2014 Media Mail
(Book, CD, DVD, Magazine)
Postal Chart

Weight not over	1st-Class w/Tracking	Media Mail Tracking w/$0.23
1 ounce	$2.32	$2.69 + $0.23 = $2.92
2 ounces	$2.32	$2.69 + $0.23 = $2.92
3 ounces	$2.32	$2.69 + $0.23 = $2.92
4 ounces	$2.50	$2.69 + $0.23 = $2.92
5 ounces	$2.68	$2.69 + $0.23 = $2.92
6 ounces	$2.86	$2.69 + $0.23 = $2.92
7 ounces	$3.04	$2.69 + $0.23 = $2.92
8 ounces	$3.22	$2.69 + $0.23 = $2.92
9 ounces	$3.40	$2.69 + $0.23 = $2.92
10 ounces	$3.58	$2.69 + $0.23 = $2.92
11 ounces	$3.76	$2.69 + $0.23 = $2.92
12 ounces	$3.94	$2.69 + $0.23 = $2.92
13 ounces	$4.12	$2.69 + $0.23 = $2.92
14 ounces	n/a	$2.69 + $0.23 = $2.92
15 ounces	n/a	$2.69 + $0.23 = $2.92
16 ounces	n/a	$2.69 + $0.23 = $2.92
2 to 70 pounds	n/a	$3.17 to $34.55
		(plus USPS Tracking)

Returns

You *must* have a returns policy. Most publishers offer a 6–12 month time span in which unsold copies may be returned to you for an account credit, or a cash refund if the books have already been paid for.

All copies damaged en route to the distributor should be unconditionally accepted for return and replaced.

Many publishers ask that customers request a return authorization number (RAN) before they return books. This helps keep inventory in check, and lets you record accurately who is returning what. Outline your returns policy clearly so there will be no misunderstanding.

Print-On-Demand (POD) books rarely allow returns. This is great for the publisher, but not so nifty for the customer. No matter— the whole deal about POD is the fact that there should never be any remainders to return, and any damaged tomes will be returned to the POD distributor. More on POD in "Part 12—The Future is Now: Electronic Publishing."

Invoice Sample

SAN 248-1707   ISBN 0-945962

Anaphase II Publishing
a division of L. Splane Diversified
2739 Wightman Street
San Diego, CA 92104
(619) 688-1959

INVOICE

SHIP TO: BookPeople
7900 Edgewater Drive
Oakland, CA 94621

ORDER NUMBER: 22524   **ORDER RECEIVED:** 6-3-94

ISBN	TITLE	AUTHOR	EDITION	PRICE	QUAN	DISCOUNT	TOTAL
0-945962-06-1	FWC	Shubailey	paper	$9.95	25	55%	$111.94

DATE SHIPPED: 7-5-94

SHIPPING CHARGE: $ 00.00
TOTAL AMOUNT DUE: $ 111.94

AMOUNT DUE IS PAYABLE UPON RECEIPT OF THIS INVOICE
or per Stipulations in Distributor Contract

RECORDED BY: _____   *Special Notes or Instructions:*

CODES:

BO	Back Ordered	
TOS	Temporarily Out of Stock	NET 90 DAYS
OS	Out of Stock	
PS	Partial Shipment	
OP	Out of Print	
PC	Publication Cancelled	
UT	Unknown Title	
NI	No such ISBN	
PA	Price Adjustment	

Billing and Collections

Distributors and bookstores rarely pay their bills without a little prodding. They've got your books, they've sold some, so who cares what happens next? *You do.*

Do not hesitate to re-bill your customer twelve seconds after the end of the grace period you've agreed upon—be it 30, 45, 60, or 90 days. If you've prepared a lucid invoice, the information has already been entered into the customer's or distributor's computer and they know very well that they owe you money. You'll have to remind them to jab their accounting department in the side. Some distributors will not cut checks below a certain amount. Wait until they owe you at least that amount, then bill them. Make sure they outline their minimum check amount policy in their contract with you.

Distributors, libraries, and colleges will almost never stiff you. Bookstores are another matter. Local independent bookstores are often teetering on the very rim of financial doom. This doesn't necessarily mean they'll do you dirt; it just means that you should pop in once in awhile and let them know you haven't forgotten about your arrangement. You might check the shelves to see how many books are gone. If it's time to collect for the books sold, do it then and there. Don't wait. I have a personal experience with procrastination: The bookstore went bankrupt after selling my books (among may others), and of course, didn't pay me for them. I lost out on both money and books—all square and legal-like in bankruptcy court.

If you have a written contract and a customer refuses to pay, you can take them to court. This is messy and prolonged but gets the job done. If you choose not to go to court, you can write the amount owed you off your business taxes as a *bad debt*—provided you have *proof* that you tried to collect (return receipt for a registered letter, or even a bankruptcy notice).

Shipping books out to unseen people is risky—especially overseas. All you have to go on is the customer's reputation in the publishing industry. Bad reputations travel far and fast, and they glow in the dark.

Pricing Strategies and Profit Calculation

Ah, yes, the old bottom line. This is where you have arrived, and none too soon. Are we making money yet?

Here's how to find out.

It is impossible to discuss profit without first discussing pricing strategies. Your cover price will be determined by several factors:

1. Cost of book printing
2. The highest discount that you must extend to buyers
3. What other books of similar quality and page-count sell for
4. Shipping costs
5. Packaging
6. Advertising and promotion costs
7. All other operating expenses including office space, utilities, office supplies, travel expenses, and professional services. You may have other operating expenses.

For simplicity's sake, let's just consider items 1–5. If you intend to make book publishing your business, you must count every paper clip as an expense that erodes away your profits. Since this isn't a business management book, we'll concentrate on general concepts only.

Items 1 and 2 are *fixed costs*—these costs do not fluctuate with the number of books you sell. Production costs and discounts are the most important consideration in pricing a book. The third item is for comparison and helps you gauge what the market will bear. If it turns out that items 1 and 2 are too high, you will have to price your book beyond what the market will bear and you won't sell many books.

Suppose you have a 64-page 5½" x 8½" perfect-bound book that costs $2.50 per copy to print in a low print-run of 150 copies.

Most books of the same quality, size, and page-count sell for $6.95 to $12.95. What should *your* price be?

Here's where discounts come into play. Let's say we have a distributor that wants a 55% discount. If you set your cover price at $4.95, you'll get $2.23. *Oops.* You're in the hole. A cover price of $5.95 will get you $2.68. At least you're 18¢ in the black. But, don't forget about packaging and shipping.

Suppose packaging and shipping combined cost about 58¢ per book shipped via the Post Office. (This is the average per book for a box of 25—the fewer books you ship, the more it costs per copy. One copy costs $1.55 for the jiffy envelope and postage.)

That brings your actual fixed costs to $2.78 per copy. A cover price of $5.95 won't cut it—you'll get $2.68 from your distributor for a book that costs $2.78 to make and ship. Ten cents in the red. Oops again.

A cover price of $6.95 will get $3.13—minus $2.78 = 35¢. Does all your writing talent, book production skills, and marketing deserve just 35¢? I hope not.

A cover price of $7.95 gets $3.58; minus $2.78 = 80¢. Not much better.

A cover price of $8.95 gets $4.03 - $2.78 = $1.25. Hmmm.

A cover price of $9.95 gets $4.48 - $2.78 = $1.70. Approaching respectability. Possibly acceptable.

A cover price of $10.95 gets $4.93 - $2.78 = $2.15. Ah, that's more like it.

The moral of the story is: Earn at *least* $2.00 or more per book for a small (dimensions and page count) book, and $10.00 or more per book for large-size, high-page-count books, and you'll make money.

Everybody gets a piece of you. Here's how that $10.95 book breaks down for everybody along the way:

The Printer makes ....$2.50..... (23%)		
You make ....$2.15..... (20%)	*Total =*	
The Post Office makes .....$0.28...... (2%)	*$10.95*	
The Distributor makes .....$1.64..... (15%)	*(100%)*	
The Bookstore makes.......$4.38..... (40%)		

The bottom line is that the bookstores make most of the money, and you do most of the work. This is especially true for low print-runs. Is it worth it? Only you can decide that. *That's publishing.*

You have yet to factor in all the other expenses that go into getting a book from concept to bookshelf. This overhead includes everything listed in item 7, and then some. These costs are *variable costs,* and you can control them with good management skills.

If you are serious about your publishing venture, enroll in business management and accounting courses. This background will be invaluable in operating your enterprise efficiently. The magic is in the details—never take them for granted.

Note:

Costs for printing are highly variable in the current marketplace. When using the formulas to calculate your profit, simply replace the figures in this book with new ones you discover when researching costs for book printing. Search for good deals (without sacrificing quality and good service, of course). Use a spreadsheet and play the "what-if" game.

Quick Tip

Promotion Basics

Talk Shows

- Be a fount of knowledge—don't be stingy and afraid of giving away your secrets!
- Make the host look like a genius for inviting you.
- Write a list of questions with short, crisp, informative answers to use as a script.
- Be familiar with the shows, hosts, and guests. Study how great guests respond and talk.
- NEVER refer to your book, a page in it, or act as if you're selling something. You are there to teach, inspire, compel listeners to want to know more.
- Speak in a friendly, conversational tone. Use humor and the WIIFM ("what's in it for me") tease.
- Find out about radio stations and their wattages: http://radio-locator.com/cgi-bin/help?topic=class
- Always follow up on guesting requests (up to 4 times), and send a thank-you note after the interview.
- Leave info with the receptionist on where to buy your book, website URL, etc.

Distribute an E-Zine

- Stick to the formula:
  - Tell 'em you're going to tell 'em.
  - Tell 'em
  - Tell 'em that you've told 'em.
- Article outline:
  - Define the problem
  - Describe what you have to offer and how it will help them. Mix modes:
    - Pain-avoidance approach: conquer, avoid, stop, relieve, lose, eliminate, overcome, etc.
    - Pleasure-seeking approach: feel, achieve, gain, have, get, enjoy, profit, etc.
  - Give the information; Sum it up
- Use information already available; simply compile and condense it.
- What do people *want, need,* and are *willing to pay* for?
- Raw material—much of it in the public domain—is available for free download from: http://digital.library.upenn.edu/books/

Media Kit

1. Press Release (1–2 pages)
2. Capsule-description (synopsis) of your book(s)
3. List of questions
4. Brief biography
5. Where to buy the book(s)

Part 12

The Future is Now: Electronic Publishing

A New Paradigm

The Small Press Comes of Age

I have good news and bad news: The *bad* news is that a great deal of what you learned in the "Color Separations," "Paper," "Printing Press," and "Marketing & Management" chapters has become obsolete; the *good* news is that the publishing world is far more friendly and cost-effective for independent and self-publishers!

Welcome to the world of electronic publishing. Even on a modest budget, you can have your books printed, marketed, and shipped—all on demand, directly from the printer/distributor to bookstores and online dealers all over the world.

Print on Demand (POD)

POD printing and distribution has and will continue to revolutionize the publishing industry. Publishers will now be able to meet demand as it arises, without investing in large print-runs or warehousing mountains of books. Books are manufactured at the time bookstores and sellers order them, and shipped directly from the manufacturer. This eliminates the need for "chain-shipping" books from printer to publisher to distributor to bookstore, savings hundreds in shipping charges alone.

The best news is that print-on-demand publishing renders the offensive "returns policy" obsolete. Standard publishing protocol allows bookstores to order books, then return them months later for a refund if they do not sell. (A recent study revealed that up to 30% of all books printed will never be sold!) This puts a serious burden on publishers' cash-flow, reducing profits and tying up funds that could be better used for business development. Print-on-demand allows bookstores to order even a single copy to test its appeal, and continue to order in small quantities until a book's popularity is well established. This is of benefit to *everyone* involved— publisher, printer, distributor, and bookstore.

Print-on-demand takes the risk out of introducing experimental titles, and allows publishers to resurrect out-of-print titles. In addition, authors may enjoy royalties for many years—perhaps indefinitely—as books need never go out of print due to low-volume sales.

Print-on-demand quality is comparable to standard printing methods, and is completely digital. The source files are PDF (Adobe's Portable Document Format), and must be set up for the specifications of the POD distributor, which varies. Books are printed on quality acid-free book paper; archival-quality paper for casebound books (when available). Binding methods include perfect (standard paperback or softcover), comb, spiral wire, case (hardbound) with jacket, and case laminate. Beautiful, full-color CMYK covers and jackets are standard.

To date, there are two major distributors offering print-on-demand technology. Though there are dozens of print-on-demand manufacturers worldwide, be aware that at the writing of this chapter, only Lightning Source/Ingram and CreateSpace (an Amazon company) include online cataloging and distribution.

POD Printers/Distributors

Ingram Book Company
1125 Heil Quaker Road
La Vergne, TN 37086

WWW.INGRAM.COM

Lightning Source POD Service
(an Ingram company)

WWW.LIGHTNINGSOURCE.COM

CeateSpace POD and Distribution Service
(an AMAZON.COM company)

WWW.CREATESPACE.COM

E-Books

Electronic books—also known as e-books—are quickly gaining popularity and acceptance within the publishing industry. Most e-books are PDF files, but Amazons Kindle format is quickly surpassing the PDF platform. E-books typically sell for one-half the cover price of the softcover edition, though prices are creeping up as the format becomes a major player in the book industry.

The two big POD distributors can make your books available in e-book format with DRM (digital rights management), which effectively copy-protects your content and keeps readers from trading with others, giving it away, copying text, or even printing it.

E-books may also be vended through a wide selection of websites that cater to self-publishers and unknown authors. Find and create Kindle E-Books at:

HTTPS://KDP.AMAZON.COM

Amazon is one of the most reputable e-book publishers, offering 35–70% royalty to the author for every e-book sold from its site. Kindle e-book earnings were estimated between $265 million and $530 million in 2013. Wouldn't you like a piece of that big 'ol money pile?

There is no charge for setting up Kindle titles—*if* you do it yourself. What follows is a short teaser-tutorial for getting your books into a format that Amazon can flawlessly convert to Kindle.

Setting Up Files for Kindle E-Books

You will set up and format your book in a word processor—no page-layout program required. Microsoft Word® seems to have the features and export filters we will need for proper file preparation, so let's play.

- ½-inch margins set as Indents; do *not* use tabs or the spacebar!
- Insert SPACE AFTER (10pts.) for space between paragraphs for flush-right paragraphs—*not* a return/enter
- Insert PAGE BREAKS between Chapters
- Do not use headers/footers, or pagination
- Images (.JPG only) inserted inline on their own line and centered. May be screen-resolution: 72–120 dpi

- Use STYLES for Chapter Headings. Headings should be assigned HEADING 1 so you can create a Table of Contents (TOC) later using this style only
- Cover image is a separate file—do *not* include it in the Word book file.
- Create Frontmatter as follows: Title/Author page (centered), Copyright Page (centered), Dedication, Preface, and TOC all separated by Page Breaks
- TOC: generate from within Word, using Heading 1 style as entry source
- Insert Table of Contents from the Insert Menu: *no* page numbers, levels = 1.
- Highlight "Table of Contents" or "Contents" in document, set BOOKMARK as TOC
- Save file as .DOC, then *Save as HTML:* WEB PAGE, FILTERED (remove Office tags = yes)
- Zip HTML file. If book has images, drag Images folder to zipped file
- Save Cover as separate file: .jpg or .tif file, maximum 1000 pixels on longest side, ratio 1.6
- Go to HTTP://KDP/AMAZON.COM and login with your usual Amazon username/password
- Upload book—following instructions—after clicking ADD NEW TITLE

More detailed instructions are available online on the Kindle site.

For a list of other e-book vendors, publishers, and free e-books, visit:

HTTP://WWW.DIGITALBOOKINDEX.COM

Required Software for Creating Digital Files for Print

Your books must be prepared professionally in a high-end page-layout program such as Adobe InDesign®, the oldy-but-goody Adobe PageMaker®, the equally obsolete Adobe Framemaker®, Quark Xpress®, or the newest arrival, the inexpensive and feature-rich Serif PagePlus®. Word processor files can also suffice, though word processors are missing some of the advanced features of a page-layout program and do not handle text as superbly as page-layout programs.

It is possible to tweak Microsoft Word®, OpenOffice Writer®, and Corel WordPerfect® to deliver better than average output for publishing.

Book covers should be designed in a high-end graphic design program such as Adobe PhotoShop®. Other design programs include CorelDraw® and Adone Illustator® (for vector-based art), Corel PhotoPaint®, and the free open-source (programmed by volunteers) GIMP, available for download at WWW.DOWNLOAD.COM and other sites. In fact, just about everywhere you look, some software company has released a graphic design program.

The cover consists of the front and back plates, plus the spine with the title. As the exact specifications for creating a book cover file differs among POD distributors, visit their websites for free downloadable templates and read the Help files for instructions specific to the POD press. It is absolutely critical that all instructions be followed, as some companies charge penalty fees for improperly designed documents. I don't know about you, but it really fries my grommets when someone profits from my mistakes....

Most high-end page-layout programs, like InDesign, incorporate routines that allow conversion of your layout files to PDF directly from within the program. You may also wish to invest in a full working version of Adobe Acrobat Professional (not just the free reader), to convert your final book-block and cover files to PDF (though InDesign incorporates a built-in routine for converting book files to PDFs). The free, downloadable Nitro PDF reader/writer will also do a nice job at converting printable layout files to PDF; no PostScript is required, bypassing an oftentimes frustrating format. These PDF files become the masters from which your books will be printed.

So, Which Company is the Best?

Compare some of the features and charges of the two big POD distributors in the table on the next page.

Bye Bye . . . Safe Journey
—Steve Tibbets

You now have a good working knowledge of book production—from manuscript to binding—and a general idea of how books are bought and sold. The only thing left for you to learn is how to endure through all of the mistakes, inaccuracies, oversights, bloopers, blunders, goofs, errors, bungles, bumbles, fumbles, stumbles, snags, snares, foul-ups, jams, fixes, spots, predicaments, entanglements, and misunderstandings that are an inevitable part of making books.

Make friends. Get other eyes on your book-in-progress when yours are too tired to see the obvious. Do things over if you have to. Accept nothing but the best you can possibly produce. Be patient with yourself and those who help you reach your goal—editors, typesetters, press people, distributors.

But most importantly—have fun. Journeys are *supposed* to be fun.

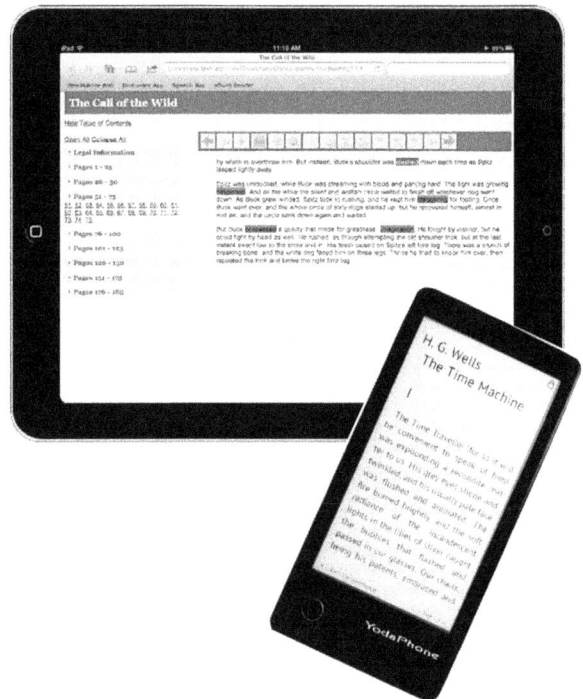

POD Specifications for a 200-page 5" x 8" Book, Retailing for $15.00

	Lightning Source	CreateSpace (Amazon)	Comments
Setup Fee	$80.00	none	
Annual Online Catalog Fee	$12.00	none	
Marketing & Distribution			
Amazon	included	included	
Other online Retailers	included	included	
UK & Europe	included	included	
E-Book Fee (prep and distribution)	included	Kindle available free, if client prepares file	
Extra Typesetting Fee (if required)	$80/hr.	variable	
Print Cost per Copy	$3.50	$3.25	
Profit on each Copy	22%—$3.25	35%—$5.25	
Returns Policy	publisher preference	no returns accepted	
Publisher Web Orders	yes	yes	
Minimum purchase	1	1	
Proof Copy Price	$30.00	$3.25 plus S/H ($0.059 + $3.00 handling/order)	
Print-to-Ship Time Frame	48 hours	1 week	
Drop-Shipping to Customers	printing/shipping only	printing/shipping only	
Payment Terms			
Books for Ingram distribution (earnings)	net 120 days	net 60 days	*payments to* the publisher
Drop-Shipped to customers/publisher	Credit Card	Credit Card	*costs* to the publisher

Book Setup

	Lightning Source	CreateSpace (Amazon)
trim tolerance	½", top + bottom	¼" 3 sides
color covers	4-color CMYK	RGB
layout page size	8½" x 11" letter	8½" x 11" letter
trim size	5" x 8"	5" x 8"
signatures	4-up	not specified

PDF File Setup

	Lightning Source	CreateSpace (Amazon)
scale	100%	100%
orientation	portrait	portrait
send image data	normal	normal
data encoding	binary	binary
embed fonts	PostScript & TrueType	PostScript & TrueType
write PostScript	PS—normal	PS—normal
composite	selected—CMYK	RGB
frequency	106	106
angle	45°	45°
text resolution	1200 dpi	300 dpi
binding	left	left
bitmap image resolution (color and B&W)	300 dpi	300 dpi
compatibility	Acrobat 5.0	Acrobat 5.0
encryption	none	none
bookmarks, links	none	none

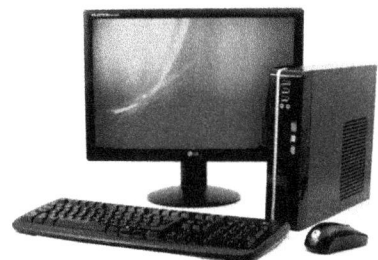

Quick Tip

Homework for the Would-Be Self-Publisher

Get ISBN barcodes and apply for a SAN (standard address number) as required in the publishing industry:

HTTP://WWW.BOWKERBARCODE.COM/BARCODE

SET UP AN ACCOUNT to print, catalog, and distribute your books:

Lightning Source   HTTP://WWW.LIGHTNINGSOURCE.COM
CreateSpace   HTTP://WWW.CREATESPACE.COM

SOLICIT OTHER DISTRIBUTORS to sell your book:

Midpoint Trade Books   HTTP://WWW.MIDPOINTTRADE.COM
Baker & Taylor   HTTP://WWW.BTOL.COM
Book Clearing House—Books, Videos and Audios   HTTP://WWW.BOOKCH.COM

JOIN PROFESSIONAL ORGANIZATIONS to help establish a presence in the publishing industry:

Independent Publishers Group   HTTP://WWW.IPGBOOK.COM
NewPages   HTTP://WWW.NEWPAGES.COM
Publishers Group West   HTTP://WWW.PGW.COM/HOME
Publishers Marketing Association   HTTP://WWW.PMA.ORG/HOME
The Association of American Publishers   HTTP://WWW.PUBLISHERS.ORG
Online Review of Books & Current Affairs   HTTP://WWW.ONLINEREVIEWOFBOOKS.COM
Publishers Weekly   HTTP://WWW.PUBLISHERSWEEKLY.COM

LEARN MORE ABOUT THE PUBLISHING BIZ *(critical!)*:

Para Publishing—Books on Publishing from Dan Poynter   HTTP://WWW.PARAPUBLISHING.COM/SITES/PARA
Poets & Writers, Inc.—Basic Info for Writers   HTTP://WWW.PW.ORG
Writer's Center Resources   HTTP://WWW.WRITER.ORG
Publishers & Writers of San Diego   HTTP://PUBLISHERSWRITERS.ORG
San Diego Writers, Ink   HTTP://WWW.SANDIEGOWRITERS.ORG

Part 13

Appendix:
Forms &
Bibliography

Feel free to copy the following sets of forms to use in your publishing enterprise.

You may also submit the forms to me for a free project quote,
or visit www.CYBERLEPSY.COM for details on my services.

Lily Splane

CyberScribe
Electronic Design and Publication Services
4669 Cherokee Avenue, Suite E
San Diego, CA 92116-3654

(619) 283-6325

LILY@CYBERLEPSY.COM   HTTP://WWW.CYBERLEPSY.COM

MANUSCRIPT SPECIFICATION SHEET

Author: _____   **Date:** _____

MS Title: _____

Corrections   ❏ replace   ❏ strikeout

Lines per page: _____

Margins in Inches   ❏ top   _____
                               ❏ bottom   _____
                               ❏ left   _____
                               ❏ right   _____

Line Spacing   ❏ single-space when _____
                          ❏ double-space when _____
                          ❏ triple-space when _____

Section Spacing   ❏ title to text   _____
                             ❏ end of topic to subhead   _____
                             ❏ between topic and subhead   _____

Titles   ❏ all caps
                    ❏ upper/lower case
                    ❏ centered
                    ❏ flush left
                    ❏ flush right
                    ❏ indented _____ spaces

Boldface Titles	❏ yes	❏ no	
Chapter Numbers	❏ Roman	❏ Arabic	
Underline	❏ chapter titles	❏ subheads	
	❏ words to be italicized		
Footnotes	❏ page foot	❏ end-of chapter	❏ end-of-book
Italicize	❏ titles		
	❏ subheadings		
	❏ for emphasis		
	❏ foreign words		
	❏ phrases		
	❏ quotations		
Offset/Block	❏ quotations		
	❏ speeches		
	❏ examples		
	❏ abstracts		
Page # Position	❏ top		
	❏ bottom		
	❏ left		
	❏ right		
	❏ center		
Boldface Page #	❏ yes	❏ no	

Check Spelling with _____ dictionary

Use Thesaurus	❏ yes	❏ no	
Hyphenate	❏ yes	❏ no	

Justify
- ❏ paragraphs
- ❏ indented blocks
- ❏ nothing

Abbreviations
- ❏ standard, based on _____ manual
- ❏ special, based on _____ manual

Grammar & Punctuation:

In-house style conventions include references...
1. *Chicago Manual of Style, 16ᵀᴴ Edition*
2. *Words into Type, 3ᴿᴰ edition*
3. *Merriam-Webster's English Usage*
4. *The Merriam-Webster Concise Handbook for Writers*
5. *Technical Writing Handbook*
6. *AMA Manual of Style (Medical)*
7. *MLA Style Manual (Law)*

Remarks: _____

_____

_____

_____

_____

_____

_____

_____

_____

_____

_____

_____

_____

BOOK TYPESETTING SPECIFICATIONS

Author: _____   **Date:** _____

MS Title: _____

Swiss Grids: _____

Text Styles: *see Style Sheet*

Book Page Size: _____

Signatures: ❑ 2   ❑ 4   ❑ 8   ❑ 16   ❑ 32
                         ❑ catalog/booklet

Margins: left   _____
                     right   _____
                     head   _____
                     foot   _____

Columns: _____

Column Interval: _____

Gutter: _____

Folios: ❑ Roman   ❑ Arabic
                     Font: _____
                     Size: _____
                     Style: _____

                     ❑ center
                     ❑ outside
                     ❑ head
                     ❑ foot
                     ❑ start at: _____

Running Headers:

❑ folio only

❑ book title   ❑ author name

❑ chapter   ❑ section

❑ graphic

❑ separator lines

❑ mirrored   ❑ alternate

❑ italics   ❑ bold

Font: _____

Size: _____

Style: _____

❑ no header

Running Footers:

❑ folio

❑ graphic

❑ separator lines

❑ mirrored   ❑ alternate

❑ italics   ❑ bold

Font: _____

Size: _____

Style: _____

❑ no footer

Design:

❑ initial drop caps

❑ end-of-chapter graphic

❑ bullet graphics: _____

❑ ¶ rules on: _____

❑ chapter title boxes *or* graphic: _____

❑ page number boxes *or* graphic: _____

❑ side-bars: _____

❑ watermark graphic: _____

❑ border graphic: _____

❑ page bleeds

Inclusions:
❑ bitmap line art (pen/ink) _____
❑ grayscale pencil drawings _____
❑ paintings—b/w _____
❑ paintings—color _____
❑ photos—b/w _____
❑ photos—color _____
❑ tables _____
❑ graphs _____
❑ charts _____
❑ vector graphic diagrams _____
❑ custom art _____
TOTAL: _____

Captions:
❑ numbered—sequential
❑ numbered—by chapter, item
❑ plain, no numbering

Pull-Quotes: ❑ yes   ❑ no

Table of Contents: ❑ yes   ❑ no

Front Matter Pages: ❑ Roman page #   ❑ Arabic page #
❑ no numbering

Bibliography/Notes: ❑ yes   ❑ no
❑ end of chapter   ❑ end of book

Index: ❑ yes   ❑ no

Pages in Manuscript: _____

Word Count: _____

Estimated Complete Book Pages: _____

COST ESTIMATE: _____

Cover Design

Title:
- ❑ font: _____
- ❑ style: _____
- ❑ size: _____
- ❑ color: _____

Attributes:
- ❑ beveled
- ❑ embossed
- ❑ contoured
- ❑ drop shadow, color: _____
- ❑ outer glow, color: _____
- ❑ inner glow, color: _____
- ❑ stroked, color: _____

Angle:
envelope style: _____
slope degree: _____

Position:
- ❑ top
- ❑ bottom
- ❑ left
- ❑ right
- ❑ center
- ❑ custom, described as: _____

Graphic:
- ❑ abstract background
- ❑ photograph
- ❑ color block   ❑ solid (none)
- ❑ custom artwork
- ❑ author supplied

bleeds: ❑ yes   ❑ no

BOOK PROPOSAL WORKSHEET

Book Title: _____

Subject: _____

Nonfiction: _____

Fiction: _____

Genre: _____

State the book's premise in three sentences or less. _____

_____

_____

_____

Why do you want to write this book? _____

_____

What is the purpose of the book? What goals do you hope to accomplish? _____

_____

How are you qualified to write the book (experience and education)? _____

_____

Do you need to do more research? _____

_____

What are your research resources? _____

_____

Do you need permissions for art or text? _____

_____

How long do you estimate this book will take to write? _____

Who is your target audience? _____

What other similar books are in print? _____

_____

Why is this particular book better or unique? _____

_____

What is the special sales potential of this book? _____

_____

What do you think will be the probable retail price of this book? _____

What markets have you identified for this book? _____

_____

Do you have, or can you get, comments or short reviews from colleagues and peers for use on the back cover of your book? _____

_____

Do you have a service bureau in mind for manufacturing this book? _____

_____

If yes, what signature setup do they use, and what are the margin tolerances of their press? _____

_____

Do you have distribution channels open to you? _____

_____

If yes, what discount do they require? _____

Do your distributors require you to pay all shipping costs from your location to theirs? _____

Do you have advertisers in mind to promote your book? If so, state what media: _____

_____

_____

Can you arrange for warehousing print-runs? _____

CyberScribe
Electronic Design and Publication Services
4669 Cherokee Avenue, Suite E
San Diego, CA 92116-3654
(619) 283-6325
Lily@Cyberlepsy.com   http://www.Cyberlepsy.com

MANUSCRIPT SPECIFICATION SHEET

Author: _____   **Date:** _____

MS Title: _____

Corrections   ❑ replace   ❑ strikeout

Lines per page: _____

Margins in Inches   ❑ top   _____
                        ❑ bottom   _____
                        ❑ left   _____
                        ❑ right   _____

Line Spacing   ❑ single-space when _____
                        ❑ double-space when _____
                        ❑ triple-space when _____

Section Spacing   ❑ title to text   _____
                        ❑ end of topic to subhead   _____
                        ❑ between topic and subhead   _____

Titles   ❑ all caps
                        ❑ upper/lower case
                        ❑ centered
                        ❑ flush left
                        ❑ flush right
                        ❑ indented _____ spaces

Boldface Titles   ❏ yes   ❏ no

Chapter Numbers   ❏ Roman   ❏ Arabic

Underline   ❏ chapter titles   ❏ subheads
                       ❏ words to be italicized

Footnotes   ❏ page foot   ❏ end-of chapter   ❏ end-of-book

Italicize   ❏ titles
                       ❏ subheadings
                       ❏ for emphasis
                       ❏ foreign words
                       ❏ phrases
                       ❏ quotations

Offset/Block   ❏ quotations
                          ❏ speeches
                          ❏ examples
                          ❏ abstracts

Page # Position   ❏ top
                             ❏ bottom
                             ❏ left
                             ❏ right
                             ❏ center

Boldface Page #   ❏ yes   ❏ no

Check Spelling with _____ dictionary

Use Thesaurus   ❏ yes   ❏ no

Hyphenate   ❏ yes   ❏ no

Justify

❑ paragraphs
❑ indented blocks
❑ nothing

Abbreviations

❑ standard, based on _____ manual
❑ special, based on _____ manual

Grammar & Punctuation:

In-house style conventions include references...

1. *Chicago Manual of Style, 16TH Edition*
2. *Words into Type, 3RD edition*
3. *Merriam-Webster's English Usage*
4. *The Merriam-Webster Concise Handbook for Writers*
5. *Technical Writing Handbook*
6. *AMA Manual of Style (Medical)*
7. *MLA Style Manual (Law)*

Remarks: _____

_____

_____

_____

_____

_____

_____

_____

_____

_____

_____

_____

_____

_____

BOOK TYPESETTING SPECIFICATIONS

Author: _____ **Date:** _____

MS Title: _____

Swiss Grids: _____

Text Styles: *see Style Sheet*

Book Page Size: _____

Signatures: ❑ 2   ❑ 4   ❑ 8   ❑ 16   ❑ 32
       ❑ catalog/booklet

Margins: left   _____
       right   _____
       head   _____
       foot   _____

Columns: _____

Column Interval: _____

Gutter: _____

Folios: ❑ Roman   ❑ Arabic
       Font: _____
       Size: _____
       Style: _____

       ❑ center
       ❑ outside
       ❑ head
       ❑ foot
       ❑ start at: _____

Running Headers:

❑ folio only

❑ book title   ❑ author name

❑ chapter   ❑ section

❑ graphic

❑ separator lines

❑ mirrored   ❑ alternate

❑ italics   ❑ bold

Font: _____

Size: _____

Style: _____

❑ no header

Running Footers:

❑ folio

❑ graphic

❑ separator lines

❑ mirrored   ❑ alternate

❑ italics   ❑ bold

Font: _____

Size: _____

Style: _____

❑ no footer

Design:

❑ initial drop caps

❑ end-of-chapter graphic

❑ bullet graphics: _____

❑ ¶ rules on: _____

❑ chapter title boxes *or* graphic: _____

❑ page number boxes *or* graphic: _____

❑ side-bars: _____

❑ watermark graphic: _____

❑ border graphic: _____

❑ page bleeds

Inclusions:	❏ bitmap line art (pen/ink)	_____
	❏ grayscale pencil drawings	_____
	❏ paintings—b/w	_____
	❏ paintings—color	_____
	❏ photos—b/w	_____
	❏ photos—color	_____
	❏ tables	_____
	❏ graphs	_____
	❏ charts	_____
	❏ vector graphic diagrams	_____
	❏ custom art	_____
	TOTAL:	_____

Captions: ❏ numbered—sequential
❏ numbered—by chapter, item
❏ plain, no numbering

Pull-Quotes: ❏ yes ❏ no

Table of Contents: ❏ yes ❏ no

Front Matter Pages: ❏ Roman page # ❏ Arabic page #
❏ no numbering

Bibliography/Notes: ❏ yes ❏ no
❏ end of chapter ❏ end of book

Index: ❏ yes ❏ no

Pages in Manuscript: _____

Word Count: _____

Estimated Complete Book Pages: _____

COST ESTIMATE: _____

Cover Design

Title: ❑ font: _____
                        ❑ style: _____
                        ❑ size: _____
                        ❑ color: _____

Attributes: ❑ beveled
                        ❑ embossed
                        ❑ contoured
                        ❑ drop shadow, color: _____
                        ❑ outer glow, color: _____
                        ❑ inner glow, color: _____
                        ❑ stroked, color: _____

Angle: envelope style: _____
                        slope degree: _____

Position: ❑ top
                        ❑ bottom
                        ❑ left
                        ❑ right
                        ❑ center
                        ❑ custom, described as: _____

Graphic: ❑ abstract background
                        ❑ photograph
                        ❑ color block   ❑ solid (none)
                        ❑ custom artwork
                        ❑ author supplied

                        bleeds: ❑ yes   ❑ no

Style Sheet

Book Title: _____   **Date:** _____

StyleName	Font	Point	Width	Tracking	Case	Position	Leading	Type-style	Align	Attribute	Indent	Tabs	Space Before	Space After	Hyphen

Additional Specs and Pub Data (see Book & MS Spec Forms)

Folios: Top Center ☐   Top Outside ☐   Bottom Center ☐   Bottom Outside ☐   Design Elements? Yes ☐   No ☐

Running Headers: Yes ☐   No ☐   Running Footers: Yes ☐   No ☐ see Book & MS Spec Form for complete details

Drop Caps? ☐   End-of-Document Graphic? ☐   Header Flourish? ☐   Footer/Folio Flourish? ☐   see Book & MS Spec Form

Allow Style Overrides? Yes ☐   No ☐

Allow Copyfitting Adjustments? Yes ☐   No ☐   Paragraph ☐   Page ☐   Spreads ☐   Column Balance ☐   Wherever Needed ☐

Footnotes: End-of-page ☐   End-of-Chapter ☐   End -of-Book ☐   Bibliography ☐   Index ☐

Copyright by: Anaphase ☐   Author ☐   Other ☐   BISAC: _____

CIP Data: Yes ☐   No ☐

Book Title: _____   **Date:** _____

Style Sheet

STYLENAME	FONT	POINT	WIDTH	TRACKING	CASE	POSITION	LEADING	TYPE-STYLE	ALIGN	ATTRIBUTE	INDENT	TABS	SPACE BEFORE	SPACE AFTER	HYPHEN

Additional Specs and Pub Data (see Book & MS Spec Forms)

Folios: Top Center □   Top Outside □   Bottom Center □   Bottom Outside □   Design Elements? Yes □ No □

Running Headers: Yes □ No □   Running Footers: Yes □ No □   see Book & MS Spec Form for complete details

Drop Caps? □   End-of-Document Graphic? □   Header Flourish? □   Footer/Folio Flourish? □   see Book & MS Spec Form

Allow Style Overrides? Yes □ No □

Allow Copyfitting Adjustments? Yes □ No □   Paragraph □ Page □   Spreads □ Column Balance □ Wherever Needed □

Footnotes: End-of-page □ End -of-Chapter □ End-of-Book □   Bibliography □ Index □

Copyright by: Anaphase □ Author □ Other □

CIP Data: Yes □ No □   BISAC: _____

Bibliography

1. Applebaum, Judith. *How to Get Happily Published,* New York: Harper and Row, 1982

2. Asimov, Janet and Issac. *How to Enjoy Writing: A Book of Aid and Comfort,* New York: Walker and Company, 1987

3. Balkin, Richard. *A Writer's Guide to Book Publishing,* New York: Plume, 3ᴿᴰ ed., 1994

4. Beach, Mark and Russon, Ken. *Papers for Printing: How to Choose the Right Paper at the Right Price for Any Printing Job,* Portland, OR: Coast to Coast Books, Inc., 1989

5. Beach, Mark and Shepro, Steve and Russon, Ken. *Getting it Printed: How to Work with Printers and Graphics Arts Services to Assure Quality, Stay on Schedule, and Control Costs,* Portland, OR: Coast to Coast Books, 1986

6. Bank, Clifford. *Type from the Desktop: Designing with Type and Your Computer,* Berkeley, CA: Ventana Press, 1990

7. Buchman, Dian Dincin, and Groves, Seli. *The Writer's Digest Guide to Manuscript Formats,* Cincinnati: Writer's Digest Books, 1987

8. Brady, Philip. *Using Type Right,* Cincinnati, OH: North Light Books, 1988

9. Burack, Sylvia K., editor. *The Writer's Handbook,* The Writer, Inc., 1988

10. Carroll, David L. *How to Prepare Your Manuscript for a Publisher,* New York: Paragon House, 1988

11. Collier, David. *Collier's Rules for Desktop Design and Typography,* New York: Addison-Wesley Publishing Company

12. *Committee of Small Magazine Editors and Publishers (COSMEP) Newsletter,* P.O. Box 703, San Francisco, CA 94101

13. Galasso, Al. *Bookdealers World,* North American Bookdealers Exchange, P.O. Box 606, Cottage Grove, OR 97424

14. Huenefeld, John. *The Huenefeld Guide to Book Publishing,* Bedford, MA: Mills and Sanderson, 4ᵀᴴ ed., 1990

15. *Independent Trade Report Newsletter,* 1992

16. Krull, Kathleen. *12 Keys to Writing Books that Sell,* Cincinnati: Writer's Digest Books, 1989

17. Lee, Marshall. *Bookmaking: The Illustrated Guide to Design/Production/Editing,* New York: R.R. Bowker, 2ᴺᴰ ed., 1979

18. Lutz, William. *Double-Speak,* New York: HarperCollins Publishers, 1989

19. Manhard, Stephen J. *The Goof-Proofer: How to Avoid the 41 Most Embarrassing Errors in Your Speaking and Writing,* New York: Macmillan Publishing, 1987

20. Masterson, Pete. *Book Design and Production: A Guide for Authors and Publishers,* El Sobrante, CA: Aeonix Publishing Group, 2007

21. Matthews, Martin and Matthews, Carole. *Using PageMaker 5.0 for Windows,* Berkeley: McGraw-Hill, 1993

22. *The Merriam-Webster Concise Handbook for Writers,* Springfield, MA: Merriam-Webster, Inc., 1991

23. Neff, Glenda Tennant, editor, *Writer's Essential Desk Reference,* Cincinnati: Writer's Digest Books, 1991

24. Parker, Roger C. *Looking Good in Print: A Guide to Basic Design for Desktop Publishing,* Chapel Hill, NC: Ventana Press, 1988

25. Poynter, Dan. *The Self-Publishing Manual: How to Write, Print, and Sell Your Own Book,* Santa Barbara, CA: Para Publishing, 7th ed., 1992

26. Provost, Gary. *100 Ways to Improve Your Writing,* New York: Mentor Books (New American Library), 1972

27. Searfoss, Glenn. *The Computer Font Book,* Berkeley, CA: McGraw-Hill, 1993

28. Shelton, James H. *Handbook for Technical Writing*, Chicago: NTC Business Books, 1994

29. Strunk, Willian, Jr. The Elements of Style, West Valley City, UT: Waking Lion Press, 1918

30. *Small Press Review*, 1992

31. White, Alex. *How to Spec Type*, New York: Watson-Guptill Publishers, 1987

32. Williams, Robin. *The Mac is Not a Typewriter*, Berkeley, CA: Peachpit Press, 1990

33. *Writer's Market*, Cincinnati, OH: Writer's Digest Books, 1994

www.ingramcontent.com/pod-product-compliance
Lightning Source LLC
Chambersburg PA
CBHW081506200326
41518CB00015B/2396